D1101283

COMPOSITION
IN COLOUR
PHOTOGRAPHY

WIM NOORDHOEK

COMPOSITION IN COLOUR PHOTOGRAPHY

 FOUNTAIN PRESS

Fountain Press
Argus Books Ltd
14 St James Road
Watford
Hertfordshire
England

© Wilhelm Knapp Verlag
English language edition © Argus Books Ltd
1982

First published 1982

ISBN 0 85242 749 2

page 2.
Poplars with mistletoe : taken in mist with a fairly
long exposure, this photo has a clear symmetry
offset by the bunches of mistletoe, and achieves
almost a monochrome effect through subtle vari-
ations of colour. A strong composition obtained by
deliberate cutting and subject selection.

Printed in England

Contents

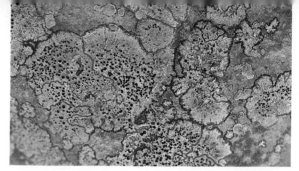

◄Children bathing in the Rio Tinto, taken from a bridge. This is a study in circles–the sun, the river, the tyre and the ripples, all linked by the golden colour of the water matching that of the sun and amplifying the circle theme.

A Friend and His Book

In the strange world of creative design, it is often difficult to distinguish between imagination and imitation. But, while it is quite clear that no work can be entirely free of either of them the question is–how can we be sure that they are in balance?

In trying to answer that question, this book does not aim to draw up geometric rules for artistic design, nor does it investigate the inner mechanisms or the functional relationships within a picture, although it does attempt to explain them. Another thing it does not do is to differentiate between photographic art and other, supposedly superior, disciplines. At the same time, it gives a thorough treatment of the basic knowledge that emerges from the analytical and constructive study of these other art forms, especially in the areas of rhythm and parallelism.

In this way, we are given important insights into the function of particular methods of design–the concept, the visualisation, and the process of optical realisation–so that we can try to bring the whole of composition theory into one all-embracing argument.

Usually photographers rely on what they call instinct to bring all the disparate elements of their composition together in the viewfinder and would 'pooh-pooh' any suggestion that they work

to fixed rules. Yet the fact is that the rules are there and they are using them, albeit unconsciously and flexibly.

For the beginner, it is probably better if he starts with some simple composition, suitable to his theme, on which he can build as his technique develops. This will allow him to keep control of his work and avoid gross errors. Only in this way will he come to an awareness of the inner forces, such as the diagonal or centrifugal constructions, which hold a composition together.

So does this mean that there will be a lot of eclectic jargon? In a way, yes, but in another way, no.

Although the intention of the book is to provide a practical guide for the reader, it will not be possible to proceed without the use of some theoretical terms, otherwise the underlying rules could not be made clear. These terms are explained in the section on photographic practice, and they are essentially similar to the terminology of colour theory. So while we will have to face some technicalities, there will be no scientific jargon!

Again, there may be some who think that the application of design only applies to certain subjects. To dispel this notion, many different subjects and motives are used in addition to the main themes which are studied in detail. And, although these photos are supplied without comment, the reader will soon realise that they are not there for decorative effect. As Wim Noordhoek has said: 'A face can be a landscape, a landscape a still-life . . . .'

And what of this man, the Author, who firmly regards himself as an *amateur* in the true sense of the word—as a *lover* of photography? After twenty years firm friendship, it would be ridiculous of me to introduce him in the usual polite phrases, as a citizen of Holland and the world, or as some sort of Aristotleian *zoon politikon*, a social animal. Wim Noordhoek, my friend and a most admirable photographer, deserves far better than that!

No, what I will try to do for him is to bridge the gap that always exists between the author and his readership. So let me begin with the words of Andy Bartels regarding the person and personality of Wim Noordhoek: 'Reflective, searching, radiating an ingenuous warmth, able to lose himself completely in his work yet sharply self-critical, open-handed, freedom-loving, full of extravagant words . . . .' For myself, I would add that Wim's speech is not arty, but powerful, and that you will find his comments on pictures always brief and to the point.

If anything, he can be too laconic, especially if there is any danger of becoming over positive about his own work. He is always wary of—if not in full flight from—anything resembling self-promotion. At the same time, his criticism is never black-and-white; he is a master of moderation, but never of mediocrity. His shorthand comments can teach you more about photography than days spent in deep discussion at some photographic meeting. Yet when he is dealing with the work of young people, he uses an entirely different vocabulary, much gentler and more cautious. For this reason, the younger generation, often in conflict with itself in trying to find its own way, takes him seriously. In his private life he is a relaxed and fascinating raconteur, the meditative side of his nature giving way to a cheerful and calm manner suffused with gentle irony. He is a fine friend and a great teacher.

As a photographer, Wim has been described as 'the old master of modern times'. He is a natural moderate who doesn't need to go in for avant-garde extremism to add to his international reputation. The 'master of soft shades and misty moods', he says '. . . you can sometimes even use full sunlight!' in talking of his attitude to the photographic image. That is his idea of extreme conditions!

So, as you can see, he is definitely not one for trendy gimmicks. On the contrary, he is the sworn enemy of outward show: in his usual rig of sweater and corduroy trousers, he would be the despair of any *modiste*! And this is not just another type of ostentation. The man is genuinely unconcerned as to the nature of his surroundings; he is equally at home in the hallowed halls of universities or in a gypsy caravan.

Open and friendly in his dealings with people, he is positively grim in his attitude to work, with an inexhaustible supply of single-minded patience when in search of a theme. Out among the Terschelling sandbanks, where most of us would see only a boring expanse of muddy water, Wim watches and waits for pictures with the sensitivity of a seismograph.

This visual ability arises of course from his origins in painting and graphic art, his skill at which is evidenced by the host of watercolours, etchings, woodcuts, drawings, paintings and graphics purchased by the Dutch government between 1940 and 1960. His works are on view throughout the Netherlands—at the Rijksmuseum and Stedelijk Museum in Amsterdam, the Boymans-van Beuningen Museum in Rotterdam, the Gemeentemuseum in The Hague, and the Prentenkabinet in Leiden. Further afield, you will also see his work displayed in the Koninklijke Museum in Brussels, the Bibliotheque Nationale in Paris, as well as showings at the São Paulo Biennale and other places.

Then, in 1956 (the year in which Gunther Anders wrote his famous essay on television with the symptomatic title 'The World as Phantom and Matrix), Wim Noordhoek became a turncoat (in the eyes of some people), and changed to the supposedly merely reproductive medium of photography. Was this just a whim, a passing fancy on the part of this multi-faceted artist? Not at all. He had in fact been receiving a thorough grounding in photography and photo-design at Dortmund under Professor Pan Walther and that free spirit of photographic art, Meinard Woldringh, now sadly no longer with us. This was of course no simple studentship. His close friendship with Pan Walther went right back to the dark days of the war when both men made known their opposition to dictatorship, and neither escaped with a whole skin.

Wim, the former motorcycle racer and track-and-field athlete is now a lover of Gregorian chant and an avid collector—the list ranges from antique toys to Greek miniatures and Asiatic artworks, not to mention his valuable books and records, of which the latter would do credit to the sound archives of a broadcasting company! All of which is kept in his old house behind Maasdijk, which looks like something out of Vermeer and is in fact protected as an Ancient Monument.

In Renaissance times, collectors were held in high esteem. Can we therefore call Wim Noordhoek a Renaissance man? Undoubtedly, because quite apart from his merits as a collector, he has been a constant advocate of world harmony, at the same time managing to avoid being a do-gooder. He is the embodiment of the philosophy of Huidinga, author of 'Homo Ludens' (Man the Player), which in a few words amounts to 'Keep it simple!' And it is certainly not simple for me to remain dispassionate in writing this biographical sketch. Nevertheless, it is time to proceed to an evaluation of Wim Noordhoek as teacher and artist. With such an individualist, all one can do is to make an attempt to relate to the present-day world, which is quite appropriate because he himself is not concerned with aesthetics in any absolute sense. For him, seeing is much more than the recognition of relationships. At a time when art seems to want to distort the world about us, or at least to represent it from some alien viewpoint, Wim Noordhoek steps forwards out of this and into a new and deeper reality.

To adapt the well-known maxim of Marshall McLuhan: 'The medium does not need to convey a message; it can also stand as a symbol of the message'. In the same way, we come to the realisation that these insights are the result of a thoroughly-researched intensification of the visible, and a spiritualisation of the forms of nature. In this way Wim Noordhoek avoids any trace of sentimentality.

If this sounds too grand, let me try to put it another way. To describe Wim's work as, 'full of penetrating detail' would be to use too feeble a phrase. It is much more like a merciless search for perfection.

On the other hand, if we look at the current scene, it is apparent that much of the avant-garde is pretentious and often clearly idiotic! Usually, this idiocy is passed off as 'art', even though nothing much has changed since Nicéphore Niépce first tried to make pictures with light-sensitive materials.

At the same time, don't think for a moment that Wim Noordhoek is looking for some lost paradise from the past or rummaging around in the attic of discarded styles, or even deliberately challenging the experiments of the present day. The point is that new insights do not arise from pulling together existing images but from being able to recognise *quality*, whether it occurs in a traditionalist or an extremist context.

This remark is aimed at the exponents of perpetual revolution, at those who have made the cult of nonsense respectable, who reject out of hand the ideas of feeling and reality and who no longer bother to consider what is aesthetically justifiable in their criticisms. What should be abundantly clear to these people from the panoramic and persuasive work of Wim Noordhoek is that discipline transcends form, that experience is greater than visual recognition, and that it is not enough merely to represent appearance – it must also be interpreted.

Of course, it is valid to ask whether Noordhoek the academic, the exponent of compositional grammar, comes into conflict with the free and unconstrained type of photography which he also advocates. Will mastery of technique, sense of purpose in composition or the rational use of the 'right' colour or the 'right' shape kill all that is spontaneous and intuitive in art? These questions might mean something if his work were to be forced into a single inflexible observer's view, or if the route from inspiration through personal conception and artistic realisation ended up in faceless objectivism. Then we could say that the result was simply standardisation, just dead photography, of which nothing more need be said.

But, in the medium of photography, Wim Noordhoek totally abolishes the 'either-or' choice between art and technique. Any possible confrontation is ruled out from the start, for an essential unity of art and technique is fundamental to all his work.

So, finally, what do we say about Wim Noordhoek and that greatly overworked formula 'magic realism'? I think we can say this: that there is nothing in this world so realistic or so ordinary, that it cannot be given a touch of poetic improbability by this man and his art.

Siegfried Merkel

Photography–
A Medium
For Our Times

SEEING AND FEELING

We go through life looking at things all the time, but looking is a passive activity. When it becomes active, and you start really *seeing*, it can be a disturbing experience. Suddenly, the thing you have been looking at – a face, a landscape, or even some minute detail – takes on a completely new appearance, moves into a completely unthought-of dimension, and appears in an entirely unsuspected relationship to its environment.

This sort of intensive looking really does open up a new world. You become like a child again, seeing things for the very first time, wandering and wondering, surprising yourself with a wealth of new experiences and a sense of wonder.

A sense of wonder is the basis of all creativity. You will want to share these new experiences with others, so you may decide to write about them. You may feel that the right medium for you would be, say, poetry. Alternatively, you may want to try to depict your new vision in paint or through the medium of photography.

Photography, after all, is a kind of language. Many photographs have simple and straightforward messages – 'This is our new baby', 'This is where we live', 'We had a wonderful holiday in Paris and here I am at the Eiffel Tower'. This is a perfectly valid aspect of photography, and is the equivalent of keeping a diary, a record of the daily events of your life. But, just as the language of everyday conversation can be transmuted into poetry, so photography can also be used to express the things that affect you deeply, things that stir or hurt, things that fill you with love or disgust, the awesome, the surprising and the lovely things of life.

Since these things and your reactions to them are in themselves out of the ordinary you must seek extraordinary ways of expressing them photographically. Here, the language of photography has its own requirements. It will require you to be bright and clear, to concentrate on the essence of the subject and to ignore extraneous material that would clutter your message. It is a language with its own grammar and, like any other language, it requires study.

But this intensive looking and *seeing*, is a gift. The things to see are all around you every day – landscape, family and the world around you, where you live and where you go. Each of us sees this world in his own way and has his own personal reactions to it. So, when we use photography as our means of expression, we must use it so that it brings out this world and the way we see it.

PHOTOGRAPHY AND THE VISUAL ARTS

In comparison with the painter, the photographer is certainly restricted. The painter is far less dependent on the subject and he can use his imagination to change what he sees, or he can use colours that differ from those in the scene before him. He can even paint from memory, reproducing a scene from childhood for example, or he can move further into the realm of imagination by painting non-figuratively, thus representing abstract ideas.

In photography, the final result is always more or less dictated by the subject of the original photograph. The eye of the camera records exactly what it sees in the form of light-rays reflected from the subject at which it is pointed. Photography is therefore absolutely dependent on light.

Now there are some art fanatics who will tell you that photography is not an 'art' at all. Well, I don't want to get involved in this pointless discussion, but I have to say that, in my opinion, there is no fundamental reason to suppose that either painting or drawing are any nearer to 'art' than photography is. Painting and drawing *can* be creative activities but that is no reason to conclude that they are *always* used creatively. Similarly, with photography there is a basic difference between using it as an art and mere visual recording.

Let's go into this a little further. There is a widespread but unthinking respect for anything done 'by hand', and especially for anything painted in oils. On the other hand, anything that makes use of some item of equipment – like screen printing for instance – is dismissed as mechanical mass-production and therefore somehow invalid. This sort of thinking seems to have arisen in the Romantic period but it is still unfortunately very prevalent.

Does this mean that mass production of replicas of the head of Nefertiti, or all the different versions of Dürer's Praying Hands, or the Van Gogh Sunflowers somehow make the original work of art any less valid? Andy Warhol's unequivocal answer to cliché-art was to raise to the level of Art with a capital A the label of a Campbell's soup-can and, by implication, anything that could be compared with it. However, many people still believe that only when inspiration wells up from the innermost being and makes its way out through the arms, hands and fingers is true art created. Why then, I ask, can't a photographer be creative when he uses his hands and fingers to adjust his lenses and press his shutter-release? Is it somehow more artistic to play a violin than to play an organ?

The fact is that if you choose your medium and work within its limitations, there is no reason why you cannot use it creatively. In other words, you should not try to paint pictures with a camera. To be a photographer is by no means to be a helpless prisoner of subject and situation. You can intervene at will, and, by choosing your position and camera angle, can alter the composition so as to add your own personal dimension to it. Give ten photographers the same subject to photograph and you will get ten different results, each with its own distinctive flavour.

There are so many possibilities. This choice, this search for a solution, for an answer to the problems set by the subject, this waiting for the perfect moment, for the light to be just right—this is where your creativity is extended to the full. You must be at one with your camera and your feelings must control the tool you are using. In this way, you can realise your own view of the world just as much as can any other artist.

What do we need?

If you want to be a photographer you will need some equipment. The question is, what? The short answer is as little as possible!

Naturally, you start with a camera. In principle, it can be any camera. You can make good photographs with the simplest type because insight and a trained eye are almost more important than fancy equipment. Put an untrained driver behind the wheel of a Rolls and he'll soon write it off!

I began with an old Ikoflex, a twin-lens reflex that gave a good big image in the ground-glass viewfinder. This had the tremendous advantage that I could see very clearly the elements of my compositions and didn't need to shuffle around here and there looking for the ideal picture. The fact is that every camera has its limitations and this is a factor which must be taken into account. Indeed, you can make a virtue out of necessity, for it is these very limitations that can force a beginner to work more positively.

Of course, as your technique improves, you will become more ambitious. Then, and only then, you can move on to more sophisticated equipment because, by that time, you will be capable of using it. Once you move into the world of the system-camera, the number of possibilities opened up is almost endless.

After a camera, you need a good solid tripod, a cable release and an exposure meter. Then—I might surprise you by saying—you should invest in some waterproof clothing, an umbrella and a good pair of Wellington boots. Photography is certainly not a fair-weather condition! Just the opposite in fact. It is in some of the most unpleasant conditions of weather that you get the lighting and atmospheric conditions which will give you the most attractive results.

So off we go on our adventure, eyes wide open, minds blank and without preconceptions. With our antennae on 'receive', our senses ready to absorb all impressions, we wait for the chance to uncover a miracle. This is where the creative work really begins.

So now we come to the 'rules' themselves:—
The first thing we can say on this subject is that the true strength of colour photography lies, surprising though it may seem, in limiting the use of colour. A feeling for colour comes not from knowledge but simply from seeing. An intellectual approach to colour blocks the experience of colour and dulls colour sensitivity.

Objective colour perception
You can start off from the simple idea that something has a colour. That it is red, green or yellow. A handy way of sticking a label on something, maybe, but not too much use for anything else. Because it is a fact that colour is not an inherent property of things. The colour you see depends on a whole range of factors—whether or not the sun is out, whether there is rain or mist about, what type of cloud there is overhead, what time of day it is, which direction the light is coming from, whether there is coloured light coming from some nearby source and a whole host of other features.

Subjective colour perception
Here, you start from what you actually experience through colour; what you select from the variety of colour and, especially, what you ignore.

In his book *The Logic of Colour*, Harald Küppers remarks: 'Ticker-tape isn't news and, in the same way, light rays are not colour. Both are media, carriers and purveyors of information.' The observer has to deal with colours that vary in brightness, purity and hue depending on their surroundings. Although it may be argued that this is only apparent, you have to remember that the colours of nature, whether perceived direct or through the medium of painting or photography, ultimately end up in the eye. It is the eye that matters; appearance is everything.

You will find, for example, that a clear red looks purplish in yellow surroundings, but that the

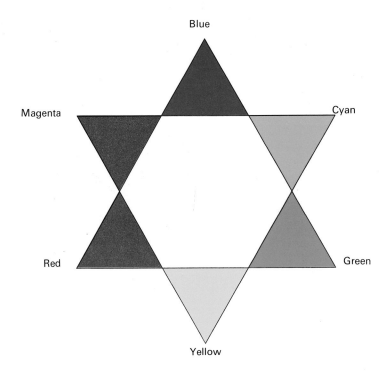

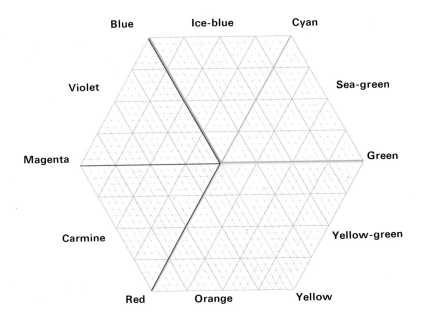

Blue is the complement of yellow.
Green is the complement of magenta (purple).
Red is the complement of cyan (blue-green).
Combination of both complementary colours will result in white light with additive colour mixing, and black with subtractive mixing.

By using various proportions of two additive or subtractive colours, it is possible to obtain a complete range of intermediate tints.

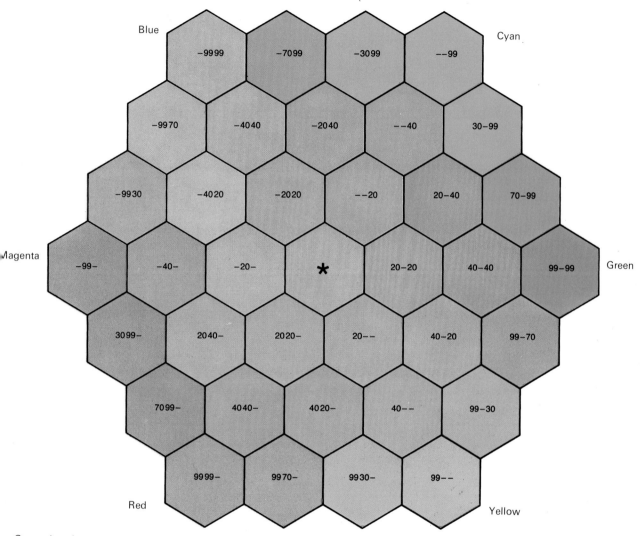

Blue · Cyan · Magenta · Green · Red · Yellow

Grey value: 1

In general, colour film is made up of three colour-sensitive layers which reproduce colours by the subtractive method. It makes sense, therefore, to classify colour-correction filters subtractively. The three primaries, yellow, magenta and cyan, are each respectively represented by a number in a group of up to three pairs, the magnitude of the number representing the filter density. So the filter combination–30–for instance, indicates that the filter colours magenta and cyan are combined.

15

same colour will take on an orange hue when the principal ambient colour is blue. It is this subjectivity of colour that makes it so attractive and inspiring to work with. Everything is changing and challenging. For myself, I have to admit that colour draws me like a magnet. The subjects that attract me do so more on the basis of colour than of anything else.

The only way to acquire a real sense of colour and an ability to react on impulse to valid colour situations is by trial and error, through many mistakes and disappointments. This is the way in which you learn to compose with the harmonies of colour, to decide whether the subject needs strong contrasts or soft pastel tints. There is no strictly scientific basis for this, because the world of colour is constantly changing; so I will not attempt to blind you with colour science. However, a little basic knowledge can help to bring some order to this world of colour, so we shall take a quick look at colour theory.

Theories and systems

The problem of colour has engaged some of the greatest minds through the ages. Books—even libraries—have been written in an attempt to classify colour harmony and in general to describe what colour is and how it occurs. Diagrams of colour systems began with della Porta in 1593 and continued through a very distinguished line of scientists, artists and philosophers including Newton, Goethe, Runge, Ostwald, Klee, Itten (of Bauhaus fame) etc.

Sir Isaac Newton, in 1660, arranged the colours in the form of a circle with white as the centre, and this was followed by Lambert's inverted pyramidical arrangement in 1772. Others have used different basic forms—Runge used a double cone (1810), Munsel a sphere (1905) and Hicketier a cube (1940), to mention but a few. This variety of approach testifies to the difficulty of classifying colour. For it is necessary not only to produce a scale of the primary colours of red, green and yellow and their intermediate tints, but also to include the subjective impressions by which one person describes ʙ colour as red, while another says orange and, still another, purple.

We will therefore limit ourselves to the very workable method of Professor Johannes Itten, as described in his book 'The Art of Colour' (1973). Our choice of the Itten Colour Circle is based on many years' experience in teaching the use of colour; it enables you to understand colour in a very accurate and practical way without the use of involved theories.

The Itten Colour Circle

The colour circle developed by Itten is 'an aesthetic theory of colour arising from experience and observation as a painter. For the artist, colour *impressions* are more important than the colours themselves as defined by a chemist or colour technician.'

It is for this reason that magenta and cyan are not located next to the primaries as they would be in a chart prepared for use in a colour laboratory.

If you look at the Itten chart shown on page 17, you will see in the centre a triangle divided into three areas, each representing one of the three primary colours yellow, red and blue. In the three smaller triangles constructed on the edges of the first one there are the three secondary colours, orange violet and green, obtained by mixing the primaries. Finally, there is an outer band divided into twelve segments, with the primaries and secondaries interspersed by the tertiaries yellow-orange, orange-red, red-violet, blue-violet, blue-green and yellow-green obtained by further mixing. Naturally, you could go on drawing an infinite number of bands with finer and finer gradations of colour on each one, but this is enough to illustrate the underlying principle.

Colour contrast in practice

The difference between colours is known as colour contrast, and it can vary from optimum to minimum.

Optimum contrast

Optimum contrast exists between the primary colours yellow, red and blue, and there is also a strong contrast effect between the secondary colours of orange violet and green. This sort of contrast can be quite attractive; it has a certain completeness about it and strong impact. Green superimposed on red and blue is often encountered in folk-art. You will find patterns in these colours on painted furniture, on earthenware, in the decorative capitals of old manuscripts, and in the borders of hand-woven cloth. Perhaps the most magnificent examples are the beautiful stained-glass windows of Chartres Cathedral—a positive vision in red, blue and green when the sun is behind them! More recently, the famous painter Piet Mondriaan in his neo-plastic period limited himself exclusively to surfaces in red, blue and yellow and emphasized the effect by the use of black outlines and white backgrounds. The advertising and packaging industries are well aware of the attraction to potential buyers of optimum contrast colouring!

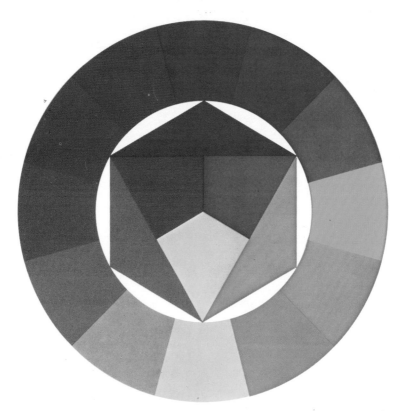

The Itten Colour circle.

If you limit yourself to optimum contrast, you certainly guarantee striking images, with a spontaneous and sometimes brilliant effect. You need only visualise the light and happy impression created by a lush green meadow with bright red poppies to realise what I mean. Or think of children clad in gaily-coloured clothing, playing with bright toys illuminated by sun shining through a window and photographed from above! There are of course some problems with the use of optimum contrast. If there are derived colours present, the harmony can be completely lost. The strong primaries lose their impact when diluted by colours which have not the same brilliance. At the same time, we must be careful not to produce too much of a good thing because this can lead to superficiality and disharmony. So, if you want to use optimum contrast, you should keep to primary colours and perhaps risk being a little coarse or even brutal, but never mix them with the softer tints.

Brightness contrast
Colours of varying strength are perceived by the eye as optical stimuli, and it is possible to distinguish between:–

a. strong and weak colours
b. clear, saturated colours of similar tone-value
c. colours of differing tone value, saturation and brightness.

The most extreme contrast is of course between black and white, between which lies a range of grey tones with lower contrast between them. However, colours also have brightness contrast. If you look at the colour circle, you will see that blue looks darker than yellow. If they were to be photographed in black-and-white, the blue would look nearest to black and the yellow nearest to white. Also, within the same colour there are degrees of brightness: pink looks brighter than dark red and would appear as a lighter grey tone in a black-and-white photograph.

When attempting to take photographs in colour, however, some care is necessary because the film cannot reproduce the same contrast range as the human eye. It is for this reason that colour photographs are sometimes a poor interpretation. In colour photography we have to deal with two types of brightness contrast: the actual contrast of the colours themselves and the contrast produced by the lighting and other ambient conditions.

Direct sunlight, for instance, can produce too much contrast by making the shadows too dark. Subjects lying close to one another sometimes cannot be photographed in strong sunlight, and strong lighting contrast can overwhelm soft colour contrast. However, we don't want to make too hard and fast a rule about the weather!

Backlighting, especially of subjects lying relatively far away, can produce outstanding results because the atmosphere softens contrast. When the sun is shining and the sky is bright, the colour expression can be intensified by means of a polarising filter. By making the sky look darker, it effectively brightens the colours in the rest of the scene.

With colour film, backlighting can be quite difficult and, surprisingly enough, some of the best results from this type of subject are obtained by the conscious use of over-exposure and un-sharpness!

Rainy conditions also present problems; the earth can easily look too dark and the colours uninteresting. In particular, if there is any part of the image where a light-coloured reflection of the sky exists, the picture can fall into two irreconcilable parts. This doesn't mean that good photographs cannot be taken in rain! However, you will need to use your exposure meter with care, taking measurements on the lightest areas and, from a compositional point of view, include the brightest colours in the area to which the main interest is to be directed. Finally, of course, don't forget your umbrella. Not for yourself – for your camera!

Warm and cold colours

When you read about warm and cold colours you might think that this has something to do with 'colour temperature'. Colour temperature is a scientific term which I do not propose to examine closely here, but which in fact has very little to do with the subjective perception of colour.

Indeed, it is almost the exact opposite of perceived colour. The colours that are thought of as 'warm' (red, orange and yellow) have in fact a lower colour temperature than those normally thought of as 'cold' (blue, violet and blue-green). This apparent paradox arises because the term colour temperature refers to the wavelength of light and not to its actual temperature. Infra-red, for instance, which literally *is* warm (it is used for cooking), has a lower colour temperature than the

apparently cold ultra-violet. If you are still puzzled, there are a number of good books on the scientific side of photography, such as 'Colour Photography in Practice' by D. H. A. Spencer or 'Colour Primer' by Zakia and Todd (Morgan and Morgan)

The contrast between warm and cold colours has been used a great deal in painting as well as in colour photography. This sort of contrast is strongest between the colours red and blue, and if you think of sunsets with brilliant red and orange clouds within a frame of dark blue earth and sky you will appreciate its impact. Another good example is when, on a brilliantly sunny day, a storm approaches. Photographs taken with the sun behind the camera, with the angry grey-blue sky as background, also benefit from this contrast between warm and cold colours. Also, water can reflect a blue sky, and provide a contrasting backdrop to warm-coloured flowers on the bank. But perhaps the effect is at its best when used sparingly. A splash of sunlight on a red roof in a village under an otherwise cloudy sky can provide a wonderful picture because of this warm-cold contrast.

The effect of colour *temperature* is often difficult to assess. Our eyes are so used to compensating for it that we no longer notice it ourselves. For instance, in photographs by artificial light, objects that look red to the eye tend to photograph as brown because of the yellowness of the artificial lighting. Avoiding this effect takes practice in observation and in trial and error. You must be prepared for disappointment. I know of one poor young fellow who took what he hoped would be a very romantic picture of his beloved at the edge of a little wood one evening. It was very effective: she came out looking like a wood-nymph—a bright blue-green colour! The photograph had been spoiled by the green reflections from the trees in the rather faint evening light.

Naturally, the effects caused by variations in colour temperature and by reflections can be turned to advantage and can produce some very interesting results. But we shall look at these again later.

Complementary contrast

The colours which lie opposite to one another in the colour circle are termed complementary colours. They are complementary in that they cancel each other out, the result of their juxtaposition being a neutral grey.

However, from a composition point of view, you can also say that they seem to fit together well— that they 'go with' one another. The sort of colour combinations I mean are red and green, yellow and violet, or blue and orange. When these combinations are used, the colours balance each other and an impression of restfulness is created. This doesn't mean that complementary contrast is in any way 'soft'. On the contrary, photographs using this sort of contrast can be very lively. It is best to look for large and clear surfaces which enhance the restfulness of these colours. The red-green contrast is perhaps most used; as we have already noted, it is very popular in folk-art and is often seen in colour photographs as well. It is a classic type of colour contrast.

The simultaneity effect

I call this an 'effect' rather than a type of contrast because there is no colour contrast as such. What I mean by the simultaneity effect is the rather mysterious way in which colours seem to alter depending on context. To illustrate the effect for yourself, take a piece of red card and place it in turn against backgrounds of varying colours. You will see that the red looks decidedly different in each case. The same applies, of course, for colours other than red.

This is almost the opposite of complementary contrast. Colour pairs that are not complementary seem to vibrate, and appear in general to want to move towards the complementary colours themselves. This of course is another effect of the human eye, which does not accept the colours as they are and tries to push them towards where it thinks they should be. This sort of contrast can produce surreal or dramatic effects, and sometimes even angry or threatening ones that can certainly be eye-catching and for this reason it is often used in advertising.

Quality contrast

At the other extreme, quality contrast is very gentle. We are dealing here with the degree of saturation of colours or the extent to which they approximate to white or grey. A colour can be defined according to how near it is to black or white, and a scale of this relative darkness is called the degree of saturation. Colours that differ very little in tone, therefore, give a very delicate contrast that can be used for poetic effects. Certain weather conditions, such as mist, snow, or low light levels can produce this type of contrast which can be very impressive. It is also worth noting that the simultaneity effect can be put to very good use here, too. The best examples of quality contrast are found in misty or snowy landscapes without sun, but you need a trained eye, a good deal of patience and a love of your subject to get it right.

COMPOSITION
IN COLOUR
PHOTOGRAPHY

Quantity contrast

Here, we are talking about the amount of colour used. This is not simply a question of magnitude because the smallest speck of a particular colour can have an effect out of all proportion to its size. It is all a question of balance.

In her book *Colour Contrasts*, Ellen Marx says: 'In order to establish a relationship between quantity, lightness and saturation, consider the six main colours set out as six complementary pairs on a neutral grey background. We would then see that the lightness of yellow was about three times as great as that of blue. This means that, for balance, there should be three times as much area of blue as of yellow. Similarly, it would be observed that green and purple were about the same lightness, with red about twice as light as blue-green.'

The most interesting application of this type of contrast is to have a large area of one colour in which there is a small spot of the contrasting colour. This spot can be a cold colour or a warm one, it can be soft or harsh, but it must in every case be in strong contrast to the main colour area. Most important of all, it must be in the right place and it need not always be red! Ideally, the situation should be such that, if this small spot of colour were to be removed, the picture would lose all its interest.

Monochrome

And so we come to the last condition, in which all contrast is reduced to the absolute minimum and the picture is essentially monochrome. It is brought to life by subtle variations of the main colour by differences in brightness. It can exist either in variations of a single colour, or be a picture made up of almost colourless tints, in which case the effect is reminiscent of black-and-white photography.

At this extreme limit of colour control, some incredible effects can be achieved – so many that it is almost impossible to know where to begin to list them. The colour chosen can be warm or cold – sepia or grey, for example – making the whole image take on the desired mood. At the same time, it should suggest emotion of a subtle kind; faint flavours that can only be tasted, as it were, with the tip of the tongue. The greatest care must be taken, otherwise the result will be just dull.

Full Sun

There is an exception to every rule, and this is the one that shows how full sun need not be disastrous in colour photography. The harsh lighting from the right, and the deep shadows it creates, activates the glowing colour and crystallises the structure of the rocks. The strong impression of depth thus created is reinforced by the exciting contrast of green and gold. The photograph on the previous page was taken with a 21mm wide-angle lens, aimed so that the lower edge of the field of vision lay about 1m (3.3ft) away from the feet of the photographer.

THE PSYCHOLOGY OF COLOUR

It is generally accepted that colour produces effects on the emotions. Colours are supposed to be associated with emotions: red for love, yellow for hate, green for hope and blue for truth. However, these colour symbols can vary from time to time and from culture to culture. The Cheyenne Indians, for instance, associate yellow with fruitfulness and perfection, while in the Middle Ages green stood for new life, and blue (just the opposite of the 'true-blue' idea quoted above) for falsehood and deceit.

In addition to the emotional effects of single colours, there are also strong associations produced by colour contrasts, for instance:—

> red for sensuality contrasting with white or grey for purity
> red for the colour of the devil and white or gold for God
> red for danger and green for safety
> yellow for cheerfulness and grey for sadness
> green for youth and grey for age

. . . and there are of course many other examples which you can provide for yourself.

We have already spoken of warm and cold colours, but there are other simple everyday associations like this. We speak of colours as strong or weak, as passive or active, extroverted or introverted, soothing or disturbing, aggressive or friendly, masculine or feminine, romantic or commonplace, fashionable or timeless, artistic or homely. We also use colours as important indicators in everyday life, for instance:—

> at sea, red for port and green for starboard
> on vehicles, red for rear lights and white for front lights
> road signs, red for both left and right indication
> traffic lights, red, amber and green for stop, caution and go
> electric wiring, red (now brown) for live and green for earth
> water taps, red for hot and blue for cold
> bank statements, red for overdrawn and black for credit.

Examples of colour symbolism abound everywhere you look. There is a 'brown-ness' about the smell and taste of coffee. You know exactly what

someone means when he speaks of a 'grey' day. We find people 'colourless' or, alternately, 'colourful'. We describe politics as red, pink or blue, a fine-looking future as 'rosy', a raw youngster as 'green', a coward as 'yellow' and a tragedy as a 'black day'.

Now of course these colour associations are at once incomplete and entirely debatable. At the same time, however, no-one will dispute that colour has a distinct effect on the psyche. Rather than continue to quote random examples from the field of application of colour psychology, let us listen for a while to the words of the experts:—

Kurt Weidemann: 'Colour is news. It informs and stimulates our visual perception. Seeing is thinking with the eyes.'

Max Lüscher: 'No-one working in the field of design can ignore colour, although it is a common mistake to think that colour problems can be avoided or difficulties of personal taste can be bypassed, by using only shades of grey. The fact is, however, that colour not only affects us psychologically but it can also affect blood-pressure, breathing rate, pulse-rate and even glandular secretions, showing how closely mind and body are interconnected. We know how great a difference there is between the experience of clear, saturated colours on the one hand and delicate, subtle tones on the other. We know how colours in the yellow-red range seem close up and aggressive and how blue-green shades look quieter and further away. In all colours, purity and saturation heighten attention and sensation.'

Fritz Seitz (on the influence of greys): 'Grey is the suppressor of emotions. Light greys are superficial, pale and flat, while darker greys are melancholy and suppressive.'

The Peacock

The first requirement for this photograph was a great deal of patience while waiting for this proud bird to display his wonderful tail feathers. Then, there was the necessity of toning down the mesh effect of the feathers themselves, so that the second requirement was the greatest possible aperture. The third requirement was of course the desired composition.

The most important design elements in this picture give optimum symmetry, and the two compositional elements which play the most important parts are the arrangement of 'eyes' in a great circle on the tail, plus the relationship between them and the out-of-focus structure of tail-feathers. These lines all run out from a single point, like a sort of silent explosion. Finally, the centre of the composition lies below the centre of the picture thus assuring a certain stress.

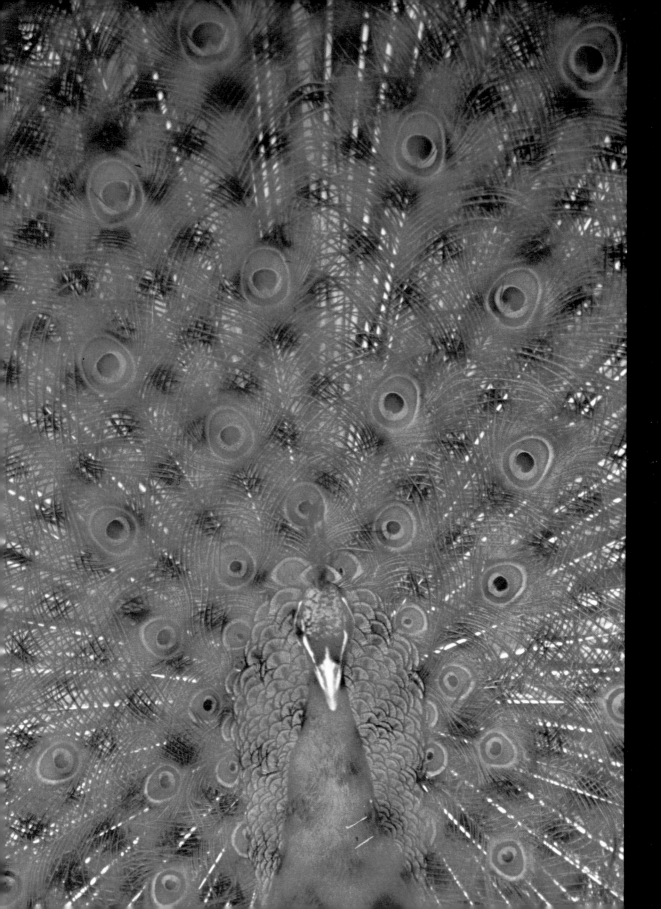

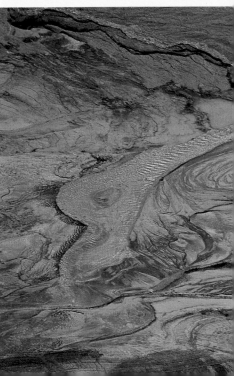

An Introduction to Design

At the beginning of this book we established that photography lends itself superbly to creative work. Therefore, design is of primary importance: what to do with your subject, how to handle it and why it should be divided in such a way. However, there is a problem. What we see has not only outline but shape, distance and depth as well. So the first obstacle we must surmount in our study of composition is to learn how to switch from three-dimensional seeing to two-dimensional thinking.

What the eye sees in terms of height, width and depth must be recreated as an illusion of space on the flat photographic image. In such a two-dimensional plane, depending on light conditions, lines and surfaces can be arranged to give texture and to produce an impression of reality.

This illusion of space can be strengthened or weakened by the use of light and shade by frontal lighting, sidelighting, or even backlighting, by choice of colour and also by camera position, which of course determines how lines and surfaces will lie in relation to the image as a whole and thus control the effect of depth. And it has to be said that not all photographers are aware of this—far from it!

If you want to work in the photographic medium, you must learn to control two-dimensionality. Only then will you know how to arrange the lights and shades, the colours, greys, lines and surfaces of your photograph to create your own personal vision.

The grammar of the photographic language

I used this term in the first chapter, and I would now like to enlarge on it a little. At colleges of art and other learned institutions where painting and drawing are taught, the starting point is usually this grammar of design. It is astounding that this is not the case in some schools of photography. It is almost as if someone wants to discriminate against photography compared with the so-called liberal arts. It is a sad fact that many of the greatest photographers, like Capa and Cartier-Bresson, had to start their training at art school. In other words, they arrived at photography via painting!

Experiments with form

Along with my students, I have developed a method for teaching design principles originally devised by my late friend and colleague Professor Röttger of Kassel. This lighthearted method uses only the simplest materials, yet is equally suitable for beginners or for more advanced students by giving an insight into the use of stress fields and the coordination of lines and surfaces as a basis for design in two dimensions.

All that is needed is a full sheet and a half sheet of white (or black) drawing paper. You cut the full sheet into 32 equal-sized rectangles. Then cut the other piece in half, and produce a further set of equal-sized rectangles by cutting one of the halves into eight. You now have 40 identical rectangular pieces of paper, and one quarter sheet which you put aside for the moment.

You will also need backing paper (black or white depending on the colour of the rectangles, to make them stand out), a sharp modelling knife, a steel ruler and some glue.

The object is to take a set of eight rectangles, cut them into two or more pieces and arrange them on the contrasting backing paper so as to form a regular pattern. As this is a type of game there are naturally some rules to be followed. The pieces of the rectangle must remain close to one another, in other words, the basic rectangular shape must be maintained, and none of the pieces may be thrown away.

Exercise 1
The first eight rectangles are to be cut into two pieces each with a single straight line. Each is mounted on the black backing paper with the two parts slightly displaced and with the rectangles themselves at a fixed distance from one another, as shown in the diagram. When you are satisfied with the result, glue the paper pattern in place.

Exercise 2
This is exactly the same as exercise 1, except that the sections are to be cut with a single curved line. To maintain a certain similarity, the cuts should intersect two sides of the rectangle. Try to keep them all different.

Exercise 3
The same again, but this time use two intersecting straight lines to cut the rectangles in four. Slightly displace the four sections to make interesting compositions and glue them in place when satisfied.

Exercise 4
This time, cut the rectangles in four using two intersecting curves and then treat as before.

In all the above examples, the sections of the rectangles should only be moved far enough to create what you feel to be an optimum tension between surfaces and lines, at which point they should be glued in place. The variations that can be worked on this simple theme are legion and,

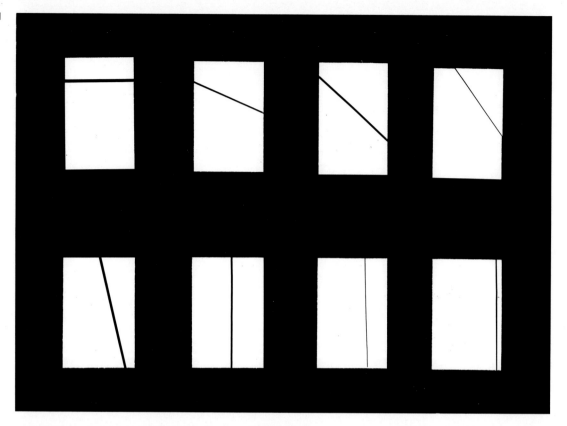

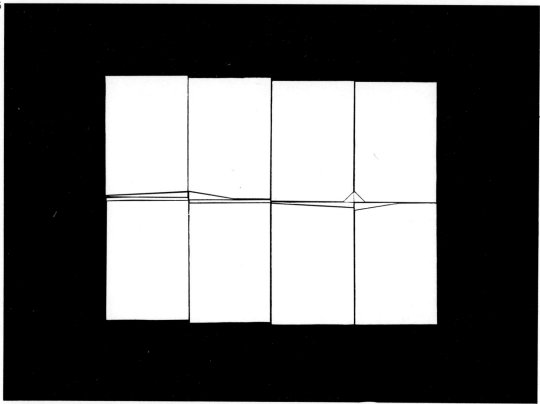

as you work, you will see that when the right level of stress is reached, blacks look blacker and whites whiter. Exercises done on different days should be compared and analysed; then when the differences are noted, you should begin to obtain a better idea of what optimum design is all about.

Exercise 5

We still have five rectangles left and these are to be cut in one of the four ways previously described (in the example on page 27 we have chosen the method in Exercise 1, but it could have been any one). This time, however, the eight rectangles are to be made into a single entity. Within that entity, the parts may be moved slightly so as to form a pattern of lines and spaces with the object of producing a single, aesthetically satisfying whole.

Exercise 6

Now you turn to the last piece of paper, the quarter sheet, and cut it into as many pieces as you fancy. Lay the pieces on the backing paper in the form of the original rectangle and then move them slightly until you achieve a composition.

The example at the bottom of page 29 shows how it *shouldn't* be done! Here the elements have been allowed to get out of balance, giving the image an unclear and cluttered appearance without any recognisable centre of sense of direction. The second example, on page 30, is much more attractive and shows just one possible way of producing an optimal image.

If these exercises are to fulfil their purpose, you must keep to the rules. In so doing, you will come to realise on analysis of your results that the strength of creative design lies in limitation. Another advantage of this type of exercise is that it can be carried out as a group project; starting with the same simple materials and using the same simple tools, obeying the same set of elementary rules, you can arrive at widely differing results and gain mutual inspiration from them.

In this way, we can learn to handle design as a sort of game. At the same time, we need not be afraid to make mistakes; we can go on moving things around until we are satisfied with what we see.

Applications to photography

The great advantage of practising with simple black and white elements like this is the development of a visual appreciation of form. The actual result obtained is less important than the process of obtaining it. Each repetition leads to more results and each is a new starting point for further trials.

But how does this apply to photography? It illustrates the principles of polarity by allowing you to handle adjacent image elements. You are presented with elements that have similar outlines, that contrast sharply with their background, and you are asked to move them about until you have found a solution that appeals to you. But what does that appeal mean? You discover the answer by doing and by feeling. You find that you can move an element thus far and no further. You are constantly faced with the problem of just how far to go, how much to do and when to stop. If you don't move the elements enough you have a clumsy lump and if you move them too much they lose their inter-relationship.

With practice, you begin to acquire an unerring instinct for the effect of form and line. You begin to see how adjacent elements of an image affect one another and how each can fulfil or stimulate the other. You realise that their positions are not just fortuitous; that force and counterforce are there and that they act against each other to produce a certain feeling of tension.

So, when you look through your viewfinder, you see not just a landscape or a face, but a series of interacting elements that can be moved relative to one another by changing your position or by tilting the camera, moving nearer or further away, raising or lowering the camera, until you have found your ideal solution. In other words you do with your camera exactly what you have been practising with your pieces of paper.

In the field, the beginner is often overwhelmed by impressions and so loses his sense of purpose in a welter of detail. With this sort of practice behind him, however, he is in a position to sort out the details and concentrate on the main compositional elements of the picture. In my opinion this type of training is not only desirable, but essential. It is the first lesson in the grammar of the language of photography.

Of course, just as in natural language, strict grammar must not be allowed to become an end in itself. It has to be used to help us bring out our creativity and to express ourselves photographically. It is a framework over which we can spread our visions so that others can see them more clearly.

The next phase in this design training programme is an experiment in pure form, for which we have an example on p. 32. This is a paper cutout by a student at the Dutch Royal Academy of Art and Design, where I teach. It is a repetitive plant-like theme in four slight variations, folded up or down, reversed, and interchanged. From this

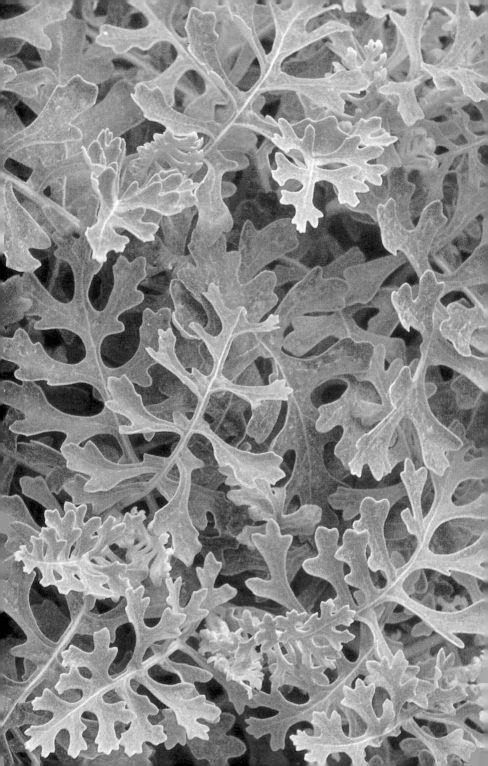

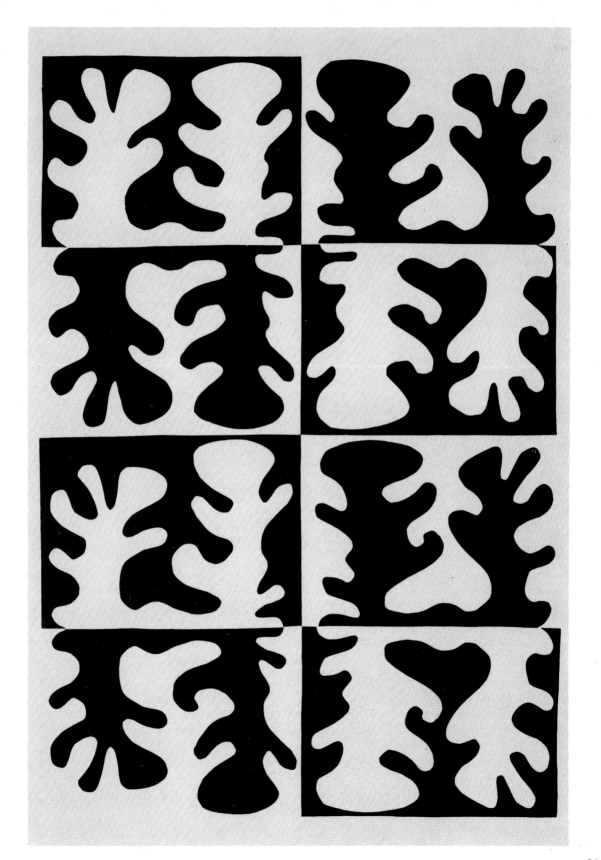

simple symmetrical approach, two different views of one object are obtained – the internal and the external forms. The themes therefore are not just repeated, they reinforce one another over the whole surface of the pattern, amplifying the graphic rhythm of the composition. The result, paradoxically, is both positive and negative.

Similar examples can be found in folk art going back thousands of years, for example, in the repeating patterns on vases or in textiles. A similar approach has been used by the Dutch designer Jos Manders in his 'Communicatie', which consists of plastic elements arranged as opposing images, the cut-out and displaced outlines of which remain in relation to one another. A photographic example is seen in the picture entitled 'Artichoke Leaves', on p. 33.

PRINCIPLES OF PHOTOGRAPHIC DESIGN

Experimenting with form is a valuable basic training by which the student comes to understand clear and rational principles on which the effect of an image depends. This knowledge can be applied to any form of creative visual art, whether it be painting, sculpture, architecture or photography.

Walter Gropius in fact laid down the basic ideas of art training for the Bauhaus using concepts from Mondriaan's 'de Stijl' movement of some years earlier. He was aiming at the unification of all craft-based disciplines such as painting, sculpture, industrial arts and handicrafts, with elementary courses as starting points. Horst Richter, in his book 'The History of Painting in the Twentieth Century' (Verlag M. duMont Schauberg, Koln, 1974), notes that Gropius set the pattern for the teaching of basic theory at virtually every modern art school and academy. However, the influence of Bauhaus books such as Klee's 'Pedagogic Sketchbook', Kandinsky's 'Point and Line in the Surface' and Moholy-Nagy's two publications entitled 'Painting, Photography, Film' should not be ignored. Overall, there is no escaping the fact that anything to do with visual expression has to do with design, and this applies as much to photography as to anything else.

HORIZONTAL AND VERTICAL FORMAT

If you are using a miniature camera, you will have to deal with one aspect of form right at the start. The picture format is rectangular and so you will have to decide whether you want the picture to be horizontal or vertical. There are no hard and fast rules about this, but if you really are in doubt as to which you ought to use, take two photographs, one each way, and leave the decision until you see which looks the better.

There are however some clear-cut choices. A landscape with some strong horizontal feature such as a river will obviously need horizontal format, thus amplifying the left-to-right motion. In general, you can say that the main line of the image will direct the choice of format, for much the same reasons. Also, the idea that horizontal format is more restful and vertical format more aggressive is not without foundation. What you must do, therefore, is to decide for yourself what you want the picture to express and choose the format accordingly.

With a 6 × 6 camera, you don't have to make this choice. However, if you change from a miniature camera with a rectangular format to something like a Hasselblad or a Rolleiflex you may find the square format rather hard to handle at first. In many cases, you will feel a need to make a rectangular picture to accommodate horizontal or vertical features of the image, and you will have to examine your transparencies critically and do some masking where appropriate.

We can't make firm rules, but square format doesn't seem to suit the human eye. However, if you feel the need to accentuate both horizontal and vertical features of the image or if you want to draw attention to the centre of the image – the point where the diagonals cross – square format has its uses (see also pp. 45-154).

Chaos and order

Anyone, whether he is painting, drawing, or taking photographs, who looks at a landscape is confronted with chaos. By this I mean he is overwhelmed with a flood of visual elements, details and situations. This is fine if you are just a nature lover; all you have to do is to enjoy it. But if you want to make a picture out of it you have a problem.

The painter always has the facility to adapt the image through the techniques available to him. He can transform the landscape into flecks of colour, lines, strokes or larger shapes and areas. In this way, he brings order to the chaotic melée of impressions that confronts him and produces his own version of it, thus communicating to the viewer what he perceives and feels.

In the same way, the photographer must produce order out of chaos and sort out a picture from the multiplicity of visual elements, using the

八日朝
打上ヶ
浪

The Wave by Hokusai (1760-1849)

to a picture, it can also make it boring! So we need a little dissonance in a picture as well.

It must be remembered that the balance in a picture is not based on the horizontal alone. Just as with the seesaw, the lever is horizontal but the motion is vertical. In the real world, the photographer stands with his feet on the ground while the sky is overhead. The picture that he sees in this way is controlled by these elements, dominated by the fall of light and by the line of the horizon. It can't be rotated. But even here we must not make taboos; in creative terms, everything that is meaningful is allowable.

Rhythm and repetition

Rhythm is a regular pattern of repetition and, just as in music, rhythm is to be found in landscapes in the form of repeating elements that bring order and stability. Rhythm connects visual elements by catching the eye, drawing it away from uneven elements and in effect pushing them into the visual background. Regular repetition has been an important style element in all cultural periods because it is an interesting and attractive feature. In photography too, the repetition of similar subjects through a picture can produce fascinating or even riveting effects. I am thinking especially of nature photography, of the natural repetition of forests, flights of gulls or swallows, or even of artificial things like the empty beach chairs after the tourists have gone home.

To quote Jos de Gruyter in his book '*European Painting in 1850*': 'Rhythm compels unity by bringing together outlying facets, by building bridges from one object to another. It unites different forms and sounds and the artist who makes us feel the rhythm in his picture also makes us realise the essential unity of things'.

Parallelism

When lines run in more or less the same direction in a picture, we call it parallelism. It has a similarity to repetition and rhythm but it is less static. Therefore it is capable of producing more fluid effects, and it occurs naturally in running water, wave-lines on sand, ploughed fields or plantations of trees. You can also see good examples of it in photographs of mudflats taken from a height.

If we use parallelism, we must remember that it is in small deviations from the exact parallel that we can introduce the most attractive form elements. Just as rhythm produces its effect by the development of a pattern of shapes, parallelism does so by the development of a particular shape. Thus there is no hard-and-fast dividing line between them; the art of the rhythmic form depends on the

techniques available to him. By the use of camera position and light, he must get rid of what he does not want and cannot use. He must balance pictorial elements like children on a seesaw, moving numbers and weights around until the distribution is even and the composition is harmonic.

In a picture, the pivotal point—analogous to the fulcrum of the seesaw is the intersection of the diagonals. Distributed around them we have the elements of the picture, trees, houses, animals or people. We can go for a straightforward balance, as with an avenue having an equal number of trees on either side. This is the simplest form of equilibrium, consisting of a symmetrical distribution of elements.

There are however more complex forms of equilibrium, but in attempting to attain it we must at the same time avoid sterile formulae because, while this will bring a sense of harmony and rest

type of rhythm and its nature.

Parallelism is enseparable from this concept. It is a 'formal relationship between various things or events lying in the same direction; a matter of similarity of direction and of distance apart.'

'The Wave', by Hokusai (1760–1849)

All this dry academic talk becomes vividly alive when we look at this remarkable representation of the wave. The artist, Hokusai, started his career as a mirror maker and eventually became the 'Rembrandt' of Japan, and even from his earliest years showed a marked instinct for the decorative as well as the correct arrangement of a pattern in a given space.

In this example of his work on page 35–one of many on the same subject–we can see how the force of the brush-stroke has been transmitted to the woodcut. The work can be evaluated in terms of accuracy, economy and expressiveness; in other words, in terms of fixed rules. Unlike western artists, the Japanese had to learn 'to distinguish the essential characteristics of the theory and basic rules that were only developed with considerable difficulty by later, modern European artists' (J. Hillier).

A further point to note in this example is the way in which painting and writing are linked in Japanese work. It is of course the Chinese characters that provide the link because they are ideographic or symbolic, thus establishing an internal as well as an external parallelism. With this in mind, you begin to understand how Hokusai was not trying to represent any particular wave, but the idea of 'wave' itself. This is how he manages to obtain such a perfect balance between the representation of reality on the one hand and the production of an attractive abstract pattern of lines on the other. Despite the almost stencil-like repetition of the curling wave-crests, this is no mere example of empty virtuosity in formal parallelism. The falling water is caught and held by the rising pattern of sign-like lines, balancing the masses and producing a bold graphic formula for tumbling water and foaming white crests. Because of the closer relationship that exists in the East between writing and painting, it is possible to achieve this translation of natural forces into elementary caligraphic language.

I suppose we might reasonably ask whether the rhythmic effect of the picture is in some way connected with the printing process used. The answer has to be no. There can be no connection between the effect and the translation from brush to woodcut, a simpler technique. Nor would it have occurred to the artist to simplify his original

Piet Mondriaan (1872–1944): Plus and Minus (1915), oils, 85 × 108cm.

drawing in order to make it suitable for printing in this way. The task of the maker of woodcuts has always been to produce a faithful facsimile of the original.

There is still another point of comparison here between the work of eastern and western artists. Surprisingly enough, a direct comparison can be made between the work of Hokusai and the pen-and-ink drawings of Rembrandt. It is clear that Hokusai knew more about European art techniques and materials than mere hearsay. In his *'Treatise on Colouring'* (1848), he writes of Dutch oil painting: 'We reproduce form and colour without relief, but in Europe they attempt to paint three-dimensionally and so deceive the eye'. Could this quotation also apply to the *trompe l'oeil* aspects of photography?

Whatever the answer to that one, Hokusai's spiritual affinity with western art is not merely fortuitous. In 1951, the National Museum in Amsterdam staged an exhibition of drawings by Rembrandt, Van Gogh and . . . . Hokusai!

LIVING RHYTHM

Although strong, clean forms have become commonplace in modern industrial design, typography and architecture, the term 'abstract art' still makes many people feel uncomfortable. This is because it lies so far away from the better-known visual language of earlier periods, such as the romantic or the impressionist. Indeed, without 'de Stijl', the Dutch art group led by Mondriaan, and their revolt against baroque subjectivity in art, and without the Bauhaus movement, we should in all probability still be in these earlier periods. There is no doubt that the 'severe' art of geometric figures has provided the co-ordinate system for the abstract design of our times.

It is perhaps as well at this point to see what the specialists have had to say on the subject of this value-free painting and to clarify matters for ourselves. For a start, we have to say that Werner Hofmann was right when he demanded a readily understandable 'colloquial visual language' for the often difficult-to-define world of abstract art. The fundamental grammar of such a language had already been laid down in the work of Klee, Kandinsky and Mondriaan. In the long term, this language is as important in its time as the theories of proportion and perspective were at the time of the renaissance.

To begin to decipher the mysterious labels that have been stuck on this type of art—the 'mystification and interiorisation' of Farner and the 'spiritualisation of matter' of Kandinsky, for example—we can look to Mondriaan himself. This theosophically influenced artist, who has in fact been called the 'Calvin of the abstract', wrote in his diary: *'Art only has meaning when it expresses the non-material.'*

This new aesthetic of the 'sacred surface', as Kurt Leonard called it, is of interest to us in the context of this book chiefly from the point of view of function. The strict order aimed at by Mondriaan was to reduce everything to the straight line and the pure surface. The end of this process is the complete invalidation of the world of the senses and the result is pure abstraction.

The line, which had formerly indicated an outline of something else, now became independent. (In the Art Nouveau period the line, which had been moving towards independence, took a turn towards the merely decorative). The concept of 'neo-plasticism' developed by Mondriaan is definitely not a three-dimensional corporality but a 'precisely reproduced aesthetic reality'. It is a new consequence of all the plastic art of the past and had occurred in painting, according to Mondriaan, 'because painting is least subject to chance' (from his book 'Concrete Art', 1930).

The character of a picture is still created by proportion and equilibrium, but what is excitingly new is that for the first time in the history of art, equilibrium is created from asymmetry and the age-old domination of static, rigid symmetry is abolished. The elements of this new painting are straight lines, verticals and horizontals, right-angles, squares, rectangles, the primary colours (red, yellow and blue) as well as the non-colours of black, white and grey.' (Horst Richter on neo-plasticism in his book 'Painting in the Twentieth Century').

Let us now look a little more closely at the detail of Mondriaan's 'Plus and Minus', recalling how the painter himself spoke of the 'denaturalisation of things'. In his book 'Abstract Painting', the art historian Lützeler had this to say: 'Mondriaan's work at first sight appears to be a playful arrangement of mathematical signs, the sort of thing that might be absent-mindedly doodled on a piece of scrap paper. In fact it is a precisely executed composition. In the lower part of the picture the elements of form are loosely arranged, while towards the top they are packed tighter. In the lower centre, we see vertical lines striving upward; but they recede near the top because now their rhythm is taken up in the whole surface; an initially isolated detail becomes as it were interconnected. Just as the picture demands that you look at it from bottom to top, so it also makes you look from outside to inside. The sharp cut-off at the edges makes the eye move towards the centre, guided by the many lines shooting towards the same central point. Yet, on the way, these lines are crossed and blocked by other intersecting lines. It is a challenge to follow this changing game of 'stop-go.'

Piet Mondriaan himself writes of 'Plus and Minus': 'The balance that neutralises and abolishes the plastic media is brought about by the proportional relationships which interrelate the plastic media themselves. These proportional relationships form a living rhythm. Every kind of symmetry is excluded.'

page 36/37.
Wide landscape in 6 × 6cm format, masked down to horizontal format. The scene is semi-backlit and the high camera position guarantees a meaningful connection of all the disparate visual elements.

Aphrodite in the arms of her mother Dione, from the east pediment of the Parthenon (448–432 BC). British Museum, London.

Experiencing abstract art in the sense of tracking down its compositional characteristics is not only a hobby for dry professionals. The previously mentioned historian Heinrich Lützeler issues the following challenge to the casual observer: 'Abstract painting invites active participation. This is a substantial part of its effect. As we begin to get the feeling for a painting's rhythms, proportions and sequences, we find that similar rhythms, proportions and sequences are being aroused in ourselves.'

RHYTHM AND PARALLELISM

The figures in the illustration above form part of a whole series of figures that together make up a total image. They come from the right half of the east pediment of the Parthenon, which excels as a striking asymmetric composition.

Taken from their overall context, there are several interesting aspects to these figures. There is a strong plastic effect, yet at the same time a striking degree of parallelism in the folds of the drapery and in the internal and external unity of the composition. The forms are of two women in a completely relaxed posture but the restfulness is totally offset by the rhythm of movement in the draperies.

This is no rigid block of stone, but a medium for a living, outward-radiating image which obtains its effect from the form, the rhythm and the flowing lines of the bodies and their clothing.

41

The impression of loosely draped material serves to accentuate the beauty of the bodies and gives the creation its fluidity.

'The formlessness of the drapery is in conflict with the solidity of the living body, flowing over it like water over stones. At the same time, it is animated and inspired with life and movement by the hidden body, without which it would merely be lifeless cloth. This combination of living body and flowing drapery triumphs over the hard stone, allowing the inner life to break out from its prison. It is the triumph of Ionic sensuality and Attic craftsmanship.' (From 'Greek Art', by R. Haman, Drömersche Verlag, Munich 1949).

This is indeed rhythm and parallelism of a high level. However, in our admiration of the ripple and surge of flowing chalk-white robes we must not forget colour. Colour? In Greek sculpture? Certainly! Despite the prevalent impression given by Winckelmann and others, the idea of ice-cold, bleached marble is nothing but a myth. There was colour, and what colour! Wax was used to colour the bodies and precious stones were set in the eyes. Just imagine these headless women as they must have appeared in their youth, radiant with colour and with jewels glittering in their enigmatic eyes.

Egon Friedell tells us that 'the Aphrodite of Praxiteles, glowing with lifelike colour, made men who saw her fall in love with her.'

DESIGNING WITH LIGHT AND COLOUR

Light

We begin by going back to our original definition of photography—writing with reflected light. If this is so, then colour photography is writing with reflected coloured light.

The great prime source of light is of course the sun that gives us all our light and warmth and makes life possible on earth. Without light, we would not be able to see, nor would we be able to take photographs. Light is necessary because it falls on an object and is reflected from it. Thus we come to the basic but essential truth: light makes things visible.

However, we could with equal validity say that things make light visible! For it is true that light-rays themselves cannot be seen; what we see is light after it has been reflected from a surface and been affected by it. It may be reflected by more than one surface on its way to the eye or the camera where it is eventually recorded.

One simple law of reflection that all photographers should be aware of is that the angle of incidence is equal to the angle of reflection.

Apart from the sun, there are of course many other sources of light. There are light-bulbs and oil lamps, fires and candle flames, as well as flash for unfavourable light conditions. The greatest fascination of photography is the fact that it is so utterly dependent on light that light becomes an end in itself for photography. The photographer has to understand how light is, as it were, captured in the black box that he calls his camera and imprisoned there until released by the mysterious forces which act to make it visible again. This is the way in which photography is creative.

However, returning to practical matters, the first thing a photographer must learn is to manipulate light, for it is only in this way that he can create. So we have to look at lighting angles. First, there is frontal lighting in which the light comes from behind the camera and very even-looking areas and soft contrasts. With side-lighting, on the other hand, the texture of a subject is brought out and strong plastic effects are achieved; the light should hardly touch the subject; only caress it.

With backlighting, there is a great deal to be obtained in terms of colour effects. Backlighting tends to intensify outlines and can thereby deepen and intensify an otherwise uninteresting subject. A landscape in mist, or even during a dust storm, can be given an added dimension by the use of backlighting, and the effect can even be found useful in portraiture.

When the light faces the lens, halation can occur and the image can be distorted with halos, reflections and star-effects. This should not always be regarded as negative; with insight and self-awareness, such situations can be turned to advantage to produce remarkable results. In creative photography, everything is permissible so long as it is meaningful.

If however you want to avoid these effects you must use a lens-hood. In some cases, the hood does not give complete protection and you may find it necessary to use your hand or a folded newspaper to keep direct rays of the sun out of the lens.

You must always be ready to experiment. What you see in the viewfinder is approximately what you will get on your film so you can assess, for instance, the effect of extra anti-glare protection. Never be afraid to make mistakes. The process of learning by mistakes is not confined to schoolchildren. The adult photographer can also learn; pondering on something you have done wrong can set you off on a new route to creative opportunities.

It cannot be stressed too often that some of the best colour photos are taken when the sky is overcast because the light conditions are very delicate and ideal for colour photography. Whereas black-and-white work depends very much on contrast, colour photographs need colour harmony.

In the studio, artificial lighting is necessary and you must remember to use film balanced for artificial light if you are making slides. The main aim should be to reproduce a natural lighting so begin with just one main light, preferably with a deep reflector. Then you will need a secondary light with a more shallow reflector to give diffused lighting, and perhaps a third light with a wide angle for illuminating the background. Avoid double shadows because the effect is most unattractive. Remember, also, that you can get good effects with only a single light-source – even a candle!

If photography is writing with light, photography in colour is much more. It is a constant struggle between the objective, scientific nature of light on the one hand and the subjective reaction in the eye of the beholder on the other. Light reflected from a surface contains certain specific colour information. For instance, the flesh tone in a portrait will be pale pink by daylight, but by artificial light it will be a yellow-red colour. However, the eye 'knows' that the colour of flesh is pale pink and sees this colour even by artificial lighting. The eye therefore does what the film cannot do – it overcomes the problem of colour temperature.

This problem usually means that film specially prepared (or balanced) for the appropriate type of lighting is needed, or that colour correction filters must be used. However, a sharp distinction between daylight and artificial light is not always possible and, indeed, in creative colour photography is seldom necessary. City shots at night, for example, should in theory be taken with artificial-light type film because the main lighting will be from street lamps. This is all very well if you want the grey asphalt to look grey and all the other colours to remain neutral. If on the other hand you use daylight film, you will find that the bluish effect it gives will improve the image of night you are trying to create and will produce attractive contrasts with the warm yellows and reds of the lamps themselves.

Mixed lighting

If there are light sources with differing colour temperatures in the same scene, we are dealing with mixed lighting. This is often regarded as a problem, but in fact the cold-warm contrasts brought about the difference between daylight and artificial lighting can produce some remarkable effects that the creative photographer can turn to advantage.

Reflections from coloured surfaces can also produce surprising effects. Take an isolated red area – by daylight it looks red but, if there is a yellow surface nearby, it takes on the warmer tone it would have in artificial lighting. The same goes for the yellow surface, of course, as it will in turn be influenced by the reflected red light. You will often find yourself being advised to avoid this effect and it can certainly be adverse in pictures of people taken beneath trees because the reflected light gives an unhealthy green tinge to the skin. At the same time, it can be put to good effect in portraits by using silver or gold foil as a reflective screen. Especially with gold foil, the skin acquires a warm and healthy look which greatly enhances the overall effect.

But it is just in this welter of cause and effect, this clash of opportunity and experience as well as the struggle between objective technique and subjective expression, that photography is so fascinating and so adventurous.

It is therefore very important that the photographer learns to see in terms of colour and to develop his feelings for colour nuances. Only then can he know for certain the differences between the colours in his subject and the extent to which they will be influenced by reflections, thereby being able to use colour effects to heighten the atmosphere and the expression of his picture.

There can be very great differences in the effects obtained by taking a photograph in the morning, in the evening or at midday. It is important to realise the effect of rain or cloud and to ascertain whether the ground is wet or dry. An early-evening landscape has dramatic impact because of the deep blue reflections from the darkening sky. Wet grass or leaves look entirely different from dry ones, while mist or rain produces a diffused lighting and also reduces the intensity of colour reflections. In a landscape with a light covering of snow, the colours can be very delicate but the contrast can be harsh. With heavy snow, there is another factor; what looks white to your eye will in fact show up as blue in the shadows and yellow in the sun, again due to the reflected-light effects we have been talking about.

With such a range of possibilities it is very easy to make mistakes, so you must be prepared for disappointment. There are many other examples of things to look out for, but we will leave them for the present and deal with them later.

The Camera

THE BLACK-MAGIC BOX

THE CONTROLS

You don't have to have an expensive camera to get good results. Even a simple camera can take good pictures. All that is needed is to know the capabilities of your camera and make the most of them.

I remember once seeing an exhibition of photographs taken by some young people who had worked exclusively with box cameras. Perhaps you remember them, those little old magic boxes? They had a fixed rectangular format, and you made your exposure by moving a lever across from left to right. There was a loud clunk and that was your photograph! Then, after winding on, you had to move the lever back again to get ready for the next photo.

Even the viewfinder was archaic–a little dim window at the top corner of the camera, through which you could hardly see a thing–although it didn't seem to be much of a problem at the time. The controls were also a little short on refinement. You had the choice of a big aperture or a small aperture and the shutter was either on time exposure or it wasn't. None of this bother about different shutter speeds!

The film wind was a real film wind, a knob that you turned until the right number appeared behind the little red window at the back of the camera. The knob would only turn one way but there was an arrow to tell you which way it turned, just in case you were too stupid to realise the fact!

Anyway, these kids had been working with this primitive equipment and you should have seen the results they'd got! There were some absolutely delightful pictures. Black magic boxes, indeed! So if you had the idea that you need an expensive wonder-box before you can start, forget it.

But surely, you will say, a little technical refinement cannot be wrong. Certainly, you get more versatility. You can do a lot more than just press a button. You can focus the lens to control sharpness, or adjust the aperture to govern exposure or depth of field. With the single-lens reflex, you can see through the viewfinder what you are about to take through the lens. Some viewfinders have built-in rangefinder devices, and prisms for precise focusing. There is automatic exposure control, interchangeable lenses and many other aids.

But, as I said at the beginning, you have to know about them before you can use them.

Let's start off with an ordinary camera and an ordinary lens. By this I mean a 50mm lens if you are using 35mm film, or an 80mm lens for 6 × 6cm. If you set the focusing scale to infinity and open up the aperture as wide as possible, say to f/2.8, you will find that everything from the far distance to something like 20–25 metres from the camera will be sharp. Everything nearer than that, however, will be out of focus. To alter this there are two things you can do:–

1. Alter the distance between the lens and the subject. If you set it on, say 25 metres, you will find that the range over which things are sharply in focus–what we call the depth of field–now extends from about 15 metres to almost infinity. Set it any less than 15 metres, and you will find that objects in the distance are no longer sharp, although objects closer to the camera will now be in focus.

2. Alter the aperture. As you reduce the aperture, so you increase the depth of field. At f/11, a lens setting of 7 metres will ensure that everything about 3.5 metres and infinity is in focus. Most cameras have a depth of field scale engraved on the focusing ring or lens barrel to help you estimate the depth at a given distance and aperture combination.

There are no hard and fast rules about this. You can get some excellent photographs at full aperture–for example backlit shots of plants and flowers, where a range of colours in various degrees of sharpness and also varying in exposure can result in a most attractive picture consisting of areas of colour against a white or light-coloured background of sky.

There are also situations in which a touch of overexposure can help. If you take a 50ASA colour film and expose it as if it were 64 or 80 ASA, the result is sometimes better. If possible, you should take a range of shots at different exposures–at the 'correct' exposure, then at half a stop over and half a stop less, and even at a whole stop less.

When you think about shutter speed, keep in mind the simple rule that a slow speed lets in a lot of light and a faster speed appropriately less. In the same way, a large aperture lets in more light than a smaller aperture. This has been taken account of in the design of cameras, where the range of shutter speeds and apertures are chosen to complement one another. For example, an exposure made at f/8 and 1/25sec is the same as one made at f/11 and 1/60, or at f/5.6 and 1/250.

This range is now standard on most cameras and exposure meters.

As you can see, distance, aperture and shutter speed are firmly inter-related. Add to this the depth-of-field effect and the limit on shutter speed for a hand-held camera (you'd better not risk hand-held shots at shutter speeds slower than about 1/60), and you begin to see the elastic but nevertheless real limits within which you will have to work.

SHARPNESS

Many people labour under the illusion that all photographs must be pin-sharp to be good. This could not be further from the truth. In a whole lot of cases, in black-and-white work as well as in colour, the use of deliberate unsharpness is not only desirable but necessary.

When taking a portrait, for instance, unwanted detail can be eliminated by careful use of aperture. With a 135mm lens at maximum aperture, you will see in the viewfinder that everything from the tip of the nose to the ears is sharp when the focus is set for the plane of the eyes. The hair and the lines of neck and chin will be slightly out of focus, and the photo will have a much more lifelike appearance with a greater impression of depth.

At the same time, distracting elements in the background can be reduced to simple areas of light and shade which no longer draw the eye away from the main subject. They can even have a positive effect in the overall composition. A lot depends on the photographer's own personal taste and on the details of the situation. There are no hard-and-fast formulae.

You can however try your 135mm lens in a different context. There are attractive shots to be had in a flowering orchard or even in the tall weeds of a grassy bank. A tripod is of course a necessity and you may need a bellows attachment for close-up work. Then you simply look for flowers, blossoms, branches, leaves or anything suitable for a subject, as long as you are 'seeing photographically' as explained at the beginning of the book.

Get close up to them. Try variations of lens, aperture and camera position. You will find that there is a whole range of attractive possibilities to be explored in every subject you choose; worlds of colour and form, some sharp, some vague and indistinct. And you will find that the hours will slip by unnoticed, so fascinating is this game of three-dimensional colours, shapes and differential focus.

Motion effects

Another reason for lack of sharpness in a photograph is relative motion between camera and subject. This happens when either the camera or the subject moves during the exposure.

As with depth-of-field effects, it need not necessarily be a fault or a virtue. A lot depends on context. If you set your shutter speed at 1/250 second, most things will come out sharp no matter what you do to the camera. But if you take a photo of a waterfall, you won't want it to look as if it's frozen. The same waterfall, taken with the camera on a tripod and the shutter set at 1/60 will look quite blurred, but it will also look much more like a waterfall with real water!

There are many such subjects to be found: trees blowing in the wind, speeding cars, circus acts, children dancing, someone talking with their hands .... the possibilities are endless. And these subjects will all look more lifelike if a certain amount of motion is retained by allowing a limited measure of motion blur to occur in the photograph.

Note that I said 'allowing'; this means that any movement that occurs must be quite deliberate and controlled. You can only learn how to use this effect to best advantage by experiment but the general rule is that the faster the motion, the shorter the exposure; always remembering that the motion must not be frozen altogether. With the gesticulating conversationalist, for instance, there is a balance to be struck between an exposure short enough to 'freeze' the person himself, yet long enough to produce an effect of motion in the waving hand.

As always, a tripod is necessary, especially at the longer exposure times. Indeed, with any lens of more than 90mm, it is indispensable. The exception is of course the shot in which the camera is 'panned', or swung so that it follows the motion of the subject. If you are photographing a galloping horse, for example, you can get all the detail you want of the horse itself with an exposure as long as 1/15 sec. Naturally, the background is completely blurred but this gives the required effect of movement.

I was once invited to the Civic Ball at the Mayoral elections in the Dordogne, in France. At about three in the morning, there was only one couple left on the floor, totally unaware of anyone else and dancing away amid the mess of empty glasses and paper streamers. The subject fascinated me and so, camera in hand, I stepped onto the floor and began to dance along with them, shooting as I went. In this absolutely bizarre situation with too little light and too much movement, I set the

the shutter on 'time' and then shot off two whole films, adjusting the exposure entirely as the mood took me. I got some strikingly expressive photographs. This is what I call having the courage to photograph something the way you see it and the lesson to be learnt from it is never to worry about making mistakes.

The many possibilities of using sharpness in your photographs can only be fully realised by experiment, by a sort of trust in the gods of photographers and by constant practice. Unfortunately, that last bit can cost you a lot of money if you use colour film. However, much of what you need to know can be learned just as well with

black-and-white film, so by all means use this to save unnecessary expense. You will be able to transfer the lessons you have learned across to the world of colour and you will have the added advantage of creating new colours by using motion blur to overlap existing ones.

LIGHT MEASUREMENT

Colour reversal film needs accurate exposure measurement. If you want to make slides you will need a good exposure meter. With negative film, if you make a mistake with the exposure you can always correct it within limits, at the printing stage. As there is no printing stage with reversal film, the exposure must be precise.

Another point to remember is that the projector you use governs the exposure you need with reversal film. If your projector has a high-powered lamp, you will need to make denser slides and you can't really tell on a viewer whether the exposure is quite right. A test projection is essential because the most interesting motive and the most artful composition cannot compensate for detail that is either washed out or swamped in deep shadows.

An exposure meter is indispensable. However, even the best meter will not work miracles for you unless you learn to use it properly. There are two basic methods of measurement:—

a. reflected-light measurement, in which the meter is pointed at the subject from the direction of the camera,

b. incident-light measurement, in which the value of the light falling on the subject is measured, using a meter with a diffuser fitted over the cell and pointed towards the camera.

The basic rule for reversal film is to measure the highlights, so that they do not appear as colourless patches when projected. If you use a camera with a built-in exposure meter, it will measure the average brightness. These meters are intended for subjects which do not diverge too much from the average subject. In other applications, such as backlit shots, snowscapes or beach scenes, where there are large areas of darkness or light, the built-in meter can play you false. Some cameras have what is known as a spotmeter and this sometimes gives better results in these cases, but you will still need to take care if the sky is too light or the landscape too dark.

You should take care not to become too dependent on your exposure meter. You will never run with crutches! An exposure meter is a very useful tool but it is quite possible to do without it in black-and-white photography. Again, bad luck can affect even the best of us and it would be a sad thing to miss the photograph you wanted just because your exposure meter had stopped working. So if you are used to relying on an exposure meter, you should try now and again to select the right exposure without it. Only in this way will you begin to develop your own 'feel' for subjects.

LENSES

If you have a camera with an interchangeable lens facility, you will also need to acquire some insight into the possibilities presented by the system. The lens you use will depend on the subjects you prefer to take. Close-up subjects like flowers and insects need a completely different type of lens from the type required for architectural shots, landscapes or portraits.

My own standard equipment is a set of two 35mm cameras, one for black and white and one for colour, with three lenses – a 21mm wide-angle, a 60mm Macro-Elmarit and a 135mm telephoto. The first of these, because of its wide field of view and large depth of field, I use for interior and landscape shots. It comes out really well for landscapes in which there is a highly-structured foreground with a deep horizon and a lot of sky having interesting cloud effects. Also, of course, it is just about indispensable for architectural work.

Used with a reasonable aperture, this type of lens has a depth of field extending from just in front of the camera right away to infinity! On the other hand, it tends to distort things. This can of course be turned to advantage: it can be used to dramatise and intensify a subject. It focuses attention on the foreground and thereby creates an illusion of spaciousness; sometimes even of unreality. With a wide-angle lens, you should be almost brutal, approaching the subject without hesitation to capture, or perhaps to create, a wonderful and quite unique world.

The Macro-Elmarit, with its 60mm focal length, is what you might call a universal lens. It is slightly longer focus than the standard 50mm lens, and has a better depth of field (1:1 to infinity), although it is not quite as fast. However, it is very versatile, allowing you to take photos close up, as well as landscapes and other long-focus shots or even portraits.

For landscapes and portraits, however, the 135mm telephoto is superb. From the same viewpoint the greater focal length has the effect of pulling the subject towards the camera, as it were, making it stand out more and perhaps providing an abstract effect. It is certainly much easier to eliminate the unwanted parts of a picture with this lens and so direct the attention of the viewer to those parts of the subject that you think need most attention.

There are of course other advantages, such as the ability to photograph subjects from a distance so that the presence of the camera does not affect their attitude. Children and animals are good examples of such subjects. Also, since the depth of field is quite limited, this type of lens is very good for subjects which need to be brought out by the use of differential focus as already described.

By now you will have realised that short-focus lenses give a greater impression of depth, while telephotos separate the subject from its environment. You must always remember, however, that it is only the angle of view that is changing, not the perspective which only varies with different distances between camera and subject.

So, finally, what should you have with you when you go out looking for photographs? The simple answer is 'not too much'. With too many lenses, selection is difficult and a good photograph might be lost irretrievably while you are trying to make up your mind. Initially, it is probably best to have only one lens and look for subjects that match it, rather than ponder on what lens to use after you find the subject. After that, choose another lens and seek out subjects that suit it and so on, until you know almost without thinking what sort of subject will suit what type of lens.

REFLECTIONS

In the section on colour, we mentioned briefly how colours are affected by reflection. This is a process that can be used effectively to obtain spectacular results in colour. Subjects reflected in glass or in water are there for the picking, boats on still lakes, a clump of reeds on an autumn afternoon or a window decked with raindrops. And the reflections need not be mirror-images; try to capture the colours of earth and sky reflected in running, sparkling water as well.

You must always remember the law of reflection; the angle of incidence is equal to the angle of reflection. This enables you to keep your own reflection out of the picture. If this is not possible use the depth-of-field effect to de-focus your image to the point where it is no longer noticeable. Often, a long-focus lens is the answer. You must also concentrate on all the compositional factors, looking at what lies to the right and left of your subject, at their colours and how

they will affect it by reflection. Wait for the right light, for the right juxtaposition of images and for the right facial expression.

Windows are subjects for detailed exploration. Think of window displays, with people gazing into them. Think of children with their noses pressed against the glass. Think of people at the windows of houses, of vases of flowers in front of glass, of curtains, of children sitting on window-sills, perhaps with pets; or even consider breaking the rule about appearing in your own photographs and do a self-portrait against some interesting subject seen through the window as background.

Once, when I was in Lisieux, Normandy, I was intrigued to find in the window of a small supermarket a cylindrical pillar covered with little squares of mirror glass. Setting up my camera with a telephoto, I was able to obtain a whole series of the market area of Lisieux as reflected in this one pillar. The smallest change in camera position produced new images—the cathedral, the town hall and the local buildings—but splintered and disorientated in an interesting way.

After a while the owner, seeing a crowd outside emerged to find out what was happening. There was this photographer taking shots of his shop window. But I hastened to explain what I was doing and even invited him to take a look into the viewfinder and see what I was photographing. I will never forget his expression of amazement when he saw in his own shop window, not the cans and boxes he was expecting, but a complete series of images the existence of which he had never suspected!

STRUCTURES AND TEXTURES

Here again there is a whole world of possibility, but you must be prepared to use your newly-acquired photographic vision. The smallest things that normally pass unnoticed, even the ground under your feet, can provide the most beautiful textures when correctly photographed. Obviously, for such subjects, a close-up lens is needed because you must get really close to the surface before the texture shows itself. Good lighting is also necessary, but too much sunlight is not a good thing as the harsh shadows often look bad on colour material. Shadows can be used for special effects, but that depends on the subject and on your own personal taste. Look also at weathering, erosion or small growths of algae or fungus, all of which can add to the interest of your macro-photograph. Structures lie on the surface of things, but they control the nature of the object and they are organic in themselves.

In fact, structures and textures have much in common. If you take an aerial photograph on a clear day, you will see far below you the structure of the landscape. You will get excellent results from an ordinary 50 or 60mm lens if you take care not to include the window-frame in shot. Back-lighting doesn't work very well in these circumstances so choose your position by the window with care.

I like photographs showing up the structure and texture of landscape and I often climb hills to take a series of photos of a particular area, using different lenses to get different effects. Naturally, I always use my tripod! The only thing to watch out for is a tendency to over-expose, so keep your exposures on the short side.

PEOPLE AS SUBJECTS

Although the black-and-white medium presents difficulties for the photographer when he uses people as his subjects, colour demands even more skill. For this reason, I think it is best to take a lot of black-and-white photographs of people before moving on to colour. It is most important to develop a relationship with the people you are photographing and it doesn't matter whether you love them or loath them as long as you have some feeling to express through the medium of colour. I am not now talking about portraiture but about taking photographs of people in a natural setting. This is what you might call 'candid camera' work; photographing people in real-life situations. This often produces the best photograph of all.

However, I don't recommend that you take pictures of people without their knowing it. It amounts to taking something that doesn't belong to you. In any case, the most fascinating aspect of photographing people, I find, is actually setting up the photograph, directing them like actors, in fact. The problem is always to get them looking natural for the camera. Out of this intercommunication arises a natural tension which eventually reaches the point of optimum relationship, and it is precisely then that the photograph must be taken.

Gypsy camp at sundown. The low sun is used to give ▶ a harsh sidelit effect. The woman at the centre is the main point of focus. The head of the little girl has been sacrificed for the sake of the overall composition. Fortunately there is no death penalty for this!

54

To help this co-operation, I often take an instant picture camera with me. I can then give my victims a print straight away, thereby building up a favourable working climate and a good understanding.

When working with colour, you will find that it plays a considerable part in heightening the emotional impact of the picture. You must therefore realise that when you photograph people in colour, it is the colour that dictates the situation. And of course, it plays a vital part in the relationship between photographer and subject which we were considering.

Another way of keeping up this relationship is not to get too far away from your subject. Your best lens is therefore a wide-angle, or at least a lens of not too great a focal length. By keeping close to the subject you retain the contact that is essential for a good working relationship. However, this is not a hard-and-fast rule. There are certainly times when a good telephoto is absolutely necessary – markets, carnivals, playgrounds or anywhere where people gather in crowds. In such cases, you don't have to worry over much about contact, just get in there and take your pictures. But at the same time be a little choosy about who, what and where you photograph.

The great advantage of photography in comparison with painting is that, in the camera, you can capture one particular moment in time. Reportage is therefore an ideal outlet. You can take a series of photographs on a given theme and tell a story in pictures. You can make it the story of a journey if you like. Whatever you do, you should if possible prepare a shooting script with a beginning, a middle and an end as well as a message or central theme. Then let the pictures speak for themselves.

SUPERIMPOSITION

When playing about with exposure or experimenting with depth-of-field effects you can produce some interesting results. It is possible to extend these even further by using superimposition. If you take two slides that are both overexposed by one stop, and superimpose them, some interesting effects can result. If the subject is a wrecked car, for example, you can give an effect of motion to it by superimposing the two slides and displacing them slightly.

EXERCISES

In this second series of exercises, you should now try to bring the most important compositional elements and groups of motives into your pictures. It is therefore of less importance to seek out particular subjects than to make sure that the theme of the exercise is fully worked out.

1. Theme : colour contrast
Use the approach described in the section on colour to produce examples of :–
brightness contrast ;
complementary contrast ; quantity contrast ;
minimal colour contrast : in other words, produce an example that is nearly monochrome.

2. Theme : elements of design
Produce some photographs in which similar design elements are juxtaposed, eg :–
large and small areas ; coarse and fine lines ;
light and dark areas in simple subjects ;
Choose a landscape and photograph it several times, moving the camera position both horizontally and vertically to get different results.

3. Theme : horizons
Choose a landscape with a clear horizon and photograph it with the horizon at various heights ; also try leaving the horizon out altogether.

4. Theme : format
Photograph various motives in both horizontal and vertical format, as well as in square format. Compare and analyse the results.

5. Theme : rhythm
Choose subjects with a repeating theme : electricity pylons, plant-life, etc. Use full format ; a telephoto will help in this respect.

6. Theme : parallelism
Look for a subject with strong parallel lines : ploughed fields, pipelines or windows in blocks of flats. Use both horizontal and vertical format.

7. Theme : reflections
Restrict yourself to a couple of clear-cut situations and then take a lot of photographs of them. Use your living-room window or try a shop window, perhaps during a shower of rain. Concentrate on colour composition and on the tension between the most abstract forms. And try one reflected self-portrait !

8. Theme : lighting
Choose subjects that are capable of being viewed from all directions, such as grasses, sand structures, street-scenes, cornfields etc : and take them with the light coming from different sides. Make

sure you get examples of frontal, side and back-lighting.

9. *Theme : colour temperature*
Choose a subject—something as simple as the view from your front window will do—and photograph it in the morning, at midday, in the afternoon and in the evening. Try it also in different weather conditions—rain, sun, mist and snow.

10. *Theme : depth of field*
Choose a subject with depth such as the foliage of a tree or shrub, and make a series of photographs using various apertures, focusing on one small detail. Get as many variations as possible using different degrees of differential focus.

11. *Theme : movement*
Try photographing a landscape with trees in a strong wind. Use various shutter speeds for each shot and make notes for comparison with results later.

12. *Theme : panning*
Follow a fast moving subject such as a galloping horse or a train with the camera and photograph it using a relatively long exposure (say 1/60 or 1/125 sec). Practise swinging the camera evenly so that the subject remains sharp against a blurred background.

13. *Theme : still life*
a. Composed still life: begin with just a few elements and try to make sure that forms and colours balance. Select the right film and exposure. Make variations on exposure and lighting.
b. Fortuitous still life: look out for suitable subjects—in the garden, in the scrapyard, by the canal or even in the graveyard.

OFF-LEVEL SHOTS

The pictures below were taken in the late afternoon. In the first one, the sun was partly behind a hill so that the garden was mainly, but not completely, in shadow. In the second one the shadow was complete. The point of the exercise, is to show how a small alteration in the position of the camera can have a dramatic effect.

Landscapes

TWO SHOTS FROM A BRIDGE

The lighting was ideal for these two photographs
—no sun and thus no reflections from the water
surface to interfere with the composition. Looking at the long and narrow shape of the vessels, a
vertical format seemed the obvious one to use.
However, second thoughts are sometimes best
and it rapidly became clear to me that with a
vertical format there was no possibility of getting
a meaningful, attractive distribution of surfaces
within the composition.

I therefore took the first photograph in a horizontal format. The motorised barge at the right is
describing an arc around the other ship, as
indicated by its wake. The centre of this circle
lies at the top left of the picture area, thereby
connecting the areas and producing stress between
them. The stress is amplified by the parallel
lines of the wash from the two ships, one set
lying at the bottom right-hand corner and the
other at the far left centre. Finally, the wake of
the smaller barge slices right through the middle
of the picture area.

Just to make sure, and as a basis for comparison,
I took the second shot in vertical format. Here
there is no longer any stress. This is due not only
to the distance between the ships themselves
but to the lack of any formal division of surfaces.
You can see this for yourself if you cover up part

of the first photograph so that only the ships themselves are visible; the picture then becomes one in vertical format.

HEIGHT

You can make deliberate use of lines of perspective to add height and distance to a picture. The things to aim at are symmetry and a use of the mid-point as a base for perspective. In the example above, foreshortened lines of perspective lead the eye from the corners of the picture into the nucleus. There, the subdued green creates an area of rest which balances the composition.

This example also serves as an exception to a well-known rule; vertical format need not always suggest activity. A symmetrical row of trees all straining upward would be unthinkable in a square format.

It is also worth noting that, while symmetry can be harmonious it may also be lacking in tension and can rapidly degenerate into meaningless pattern. The photograph above would be simply monotonous without the group of sheep at the centre. The thin branch straying across the avenue of trees also helps.

The photographer has the task of portraying a three-dimensional world on a two-dimensional surface. Perhaps the main lesson to be learnt here is that, although all the elements are shown in sharp focus by the use of the space shrinking telephoto lens, the impression of depth has still been maintained. Again, proof that there is an exception to every rule.

HORIZON AND CONTRAST

Technique and composition can be learnt. They are the result of a sort of aesthetic production line. But, although they are important as intermediate stages in the creative process, without the initial creative imagination they are nothing.

At the same time, we also have to remember that pictures of 'nice-looking things' made without reference to the basic rules of design are often no more than laudable efforts. These considerations lead to the important question of whether one should approach a subject 'intuitively' or 'professionally'. I might add that this problem is something that every photographer, and not only amateurs, has to face quite often.

However, that was fortunately not the case with me when I took the photograph on the left, a landscape of Lüneburg Heath in Germany. It was just a case of looking in the viewfinder, peering here and there for a minute or so, and then that wonderful feeling of 'this is it!' Afterwards, I had to look at the print and see just what the 'it' had been.

The principal feature is the little pathway that winds slowly from bottom left to top right. The bends are unevenly placed within the picture area and the nearer one, being correspondingly flatter and more forceful, finds its counterweight in the house, which is in just the right place. The single free-standing tree just moves the weight enough to the left to balance the picture up nicely. If you cover up the house, there is nothing in the picture worth noticing – but the same applies if you cover up the pathway and leave the house, or even if you cover up the single tree. In this case, intuition said that there was no need to have the sky in the shot and, in this case, intuition was right!

It was quite different with the photograph of the dunes shown overleaf. The quantity of images of all the individual plantlets is almost confusing to the eye so some strong compositional thinking was needed in order to overcome the aesthetic and technical problems involved.

To begin with, a wide-angle lens was an absolute necessity for this width of landscape. The short focal length allowed me to use a medium aperture

so as to get a considerable depth of field and, especially, to use a fast shutter speed so as to freeze the motion of the grass plants as they bent over in the hard wind.

The second factor involved was the blue-black sky and the contrast it has with the brightly lit dune. There was no question of using square or vertical format because this would have brought the horizon down to the middle of the picture and split it in two; compositionally very undesirable. But clearly some counterweight is needed to the yellow dune, and the dark and stormy sky provides just the right contrast. So the problem is not whether the sky should be included, but how much. In other words, just where should the horizon come in the picture? Eventually I decided on the amount shown. Too much would have deadened the picture but too little would have left it without interest. Try covering up the sky to see what effect it has on the overall appearance.

The two main colours (the greenish-yellow section doesn't really do much) work well with one another, but there is yet another factor involved. In addition to the light-dark and the complementary contrast already in the picture, there is also a quantity contrast. The light-dark contrast brings out the surfaces in the picture while the complementary contrast (yellow through yellow-green to slate-blue) strengthens this through the use of colour. Finally, the quantity contrast adds yet another strength; the measuring-off of colour into the planes of the image itself.

RIGHT AND LEFT

'In spite of every theoretical and technical consideration, composition is a creative process that can never be replaced by mere calculation.' This remark is certainly true of this picture of an orchard in spring where the tension between the three trees and the primary colours of green, black and grey form the main design elements. But, in fact, this apparently creative process consisted of a long drawn-out and thoroughly boring search for the best camera position. A bit closer,

a bit further away, left a bit, right a bit . . . . on and on until there was just the right tension and the right degree of expression in the composition appearing in the viewfinder. It was, in other words, just like out exercise in which we moved the design elements around until they were just right and could not be moved any more without losing something. And is this the optimum? Well, we'll come back to that in a moment.

If you lay this photograph on a table or project it on to a screen, you can analyse it fairly easily from a compositional point of view. There are three trees which have a mutual interrelationship, and they form three points of origin for the tracery of sharply-illuminated twigs that spreads out over the whole image area. The first is the cut-off central tree which rises from the bottom of the picture and leads the eye right and towards the second, higher tree, which bends to the left. This leads the eye round through its branches to find the third tree at the far left of the picture and this neatly closes off the composition. There

are areas of restfulness at bottom left and top right, and the greatest activity takes place along the top-left to bottom-right diagonal.

But is this the only interpretation that can be made? Let's try turning the page . . . .

ORIGINAL–OR MIRROR-IMAGE?

The way in which the eye 'reads' a picture, and the phenomenon of reversibility of images are problems that have exercised the minds of artists for a very long time–back at least as far as the etchings of Rembrandt, which of course had to be printed in reverse. By and large, the conclusion has been reached that we approach a picture in much the same way as we read a page of print– moving from left to right and from top to bottom. 'The experience or concept of space', writes *Oestrich*, 'is not necessarily understood as an actual three-dimensional space.' And in '*Foundations of Psychology*' (Boring-Lanfeld-Weld,

1948), we read: 'The concept of space lies within ourselves; as far as our senses are concerned, there is no difference between real space, and space represented by a picture.'

What has this to do with the difference between these two reverse-image photographs? The compositional elements are the same in both, but the first picture looks flatter and the second more three-dimensional. The main reason for this is that the area of restfulness lies at the right of the second picture, at the end of the eye-track. However, this is only true for the observer who is right-handed! Leonardo da Vinci, who was of course left-handed, always seems to perceive things the 'wrong way round'. If his 'Last Supper' is projected as a mirror image, it somehow looks more 'correct'.

Now, of course, the question arises as to which of the above two pictures is the 'correct' one. You might like to guess before I tell you. As it happens, the original was in fact the second one, so the first one, which is compositionally better, is in fact the product of 'purely intellectual calcula-

tion'. I make no apologies for this trick; it is not just a little joke but a clear-cut example intended to give insight into the principles of design and composition that we have been discussing.

IMAGE DIAGONALS

Let's now have a look at another example of pictorial composition. Here (on the right) we have a picture of some houses in a valley, surrounded by trees and shrubbery in autumn colours. Both elements have their part to play; the square, hard outlines of the roofs are surrounded by the formless patches of colour in the foliage. Also, the row of small, bright patches at the top right, paralleling the line of the tops of the light-coloured trees lower left, is of great importance to the overall composition. This is a clear example of quality contrast, having a whole range of shades from grey to intense colours. Naturally, it was not a photograph in which bright sunlight was required!

TELEPHOTOS AND CAMERA-POSITION

The use of lenses of varying focal length can be of great assistance in the application of line-and-surface design processes to landscape photography. Short-focus lenses distort the foreground, making it look very wide and dramatic. At the other extreme, telephotos bring the background closer and foreshorten the image. This is apparent in the photograph of the Norwegian church on the previous page, for which I used a 250mm lens from a long way off in order to keep the sky out of the shot. Because of the distance the greens in the picture are tinted with blue and the hillside behind the church forms an almost vertical curtain because of the foreshortening effect of the lens. These two effects, taken together, suffuse the image with blue-green and give rise to a mixed-light contrast. At the same time, the twin spires of the church and the spruce tree to the right of it frame the large dark area provided by the copper beech. There was in fact another similar beech to the left of the church but I kept it out of shot; first of all because it would have weakened the composition and secondly because it would have allowed part of the sky to come into the picture, which as I have already remarked, I did not want.

The photograph on the facing page shows a telephoto used from an entirely different camera position. Here the effect is enhanced by the strong sidelighting which brings out the powerful perspective of the parallel lines of the furrows in the ploughed field and contrasts the surface structure of the ground with the hard lines of the buildings. If the two rectangular areas at the top right were not there, the whole basis of the picture would be too heavy. Again, the rather rigid line of the cart-track, which acts as a sort of hawser lifting the bottom of the picture upwards, is softened slightly by the gently undulating lines of the furrows. Lastly, the roof tiles, which in general run the same way as the rest of the lines in the picture, bring the whole composition to a satisfactory conclusion.

TELEPHOTO OR STANDARD LENS?

A clear example of the effect of lenses of differing focal length is provided by these two photographs of a lake with waterlilies. Both were taken from the same position, but for one a 50mm standard lens was used, which for the second

PARALLELISM

photograph was replaced by a 180mm telephoto lens with a polarising filter to keep out unwanted reflections.

The first is very reminiscent of the 'Waterlilies' series by the French impressionist Monet. The whole image seems to consist of tiny points of colour. This is how the scene looks in real life, a living example of pointillism.

The second example, although simply a detail of the first, looks completely different. The effect of the pictures is produced through the action of completely different mechanisms; in the first, through the rhythmic variation of relatively large areas of hazy colour and in the second through the distinct pattern of green and violet diagonals as well as the sharp division of form and colour.

When we dealt with parallelism on p. 35, we noted that 'it is in small deviations from the exact parallel that we can introduce the most attractive form elements.' This is precisely what we find in this study of a forest of poplars, especially in the tree at the lower left of centre and in the curving branches just to the right. There is also the slant of the poplar to the left, just touched by the outermost branch of the low tree, and the variation in the lengths of the poplars themselves.

Indeed, the caption to this picture could have been written by the Swiss painter Ferdinand Hodler who noted in his diary (in 1897!): 'Whether or not these upward-straining trees are set against a dark background or against a blue sky, their overall impression of unity owes most to their parallelism.'

SUN – OR NO SUN?

Another example of the same photograph taken under different conditions, this time showing the effect of sunlight. These two shots of the mudflats in the Wadden Sea were taken from exactly the same position, using the same lens and the same make of film. The only difference is that the sun was shining brightly in the first one and was obscured in the second. What a difference!

Strangely enough, the colour temperature of the first photograph is *lower* than the second, but that is only another way of saying that the colours are *warmer*. Not only that, the relationship of the colours to one another is completely different in the two photographs. Yet these were changes that took place within the few minutes that were needed for clouds to obscure the sun.

What is most striking is that not only are the colour relationships changed, but the shapes are as well. If you look at the first photo, you will see that the sandbank in the background seems further away and nearer to the horizon than in the lower photo. In the same way, the beach-like area in the foreground seems to stretch further seawards. Yet measurement will show that this is not the case!

So you see this change in the light gives a totally different aspect to the same landscape. The first is rather naturalistic or poetic, the second atmospheric and dramatic. Lighting, therefore, is extremely important in photographic composition, not only to produce brightness and colour but also to give shape and atmosphere to the image.

THE CITY ON THE HILL

This photograph of a hilltop city in southern Italy has three main features: structure, rhythm and light. Despite the superfluity of detail, structure is important. On the right there is a light-coloured triangle in the foreground, brightly lit by the sun and contrasting with the larger, darker triangle lying in the shadow to the left. The sun comes from the left and the triangles have contrasting diagonals. In the background, the sun-bleached city dominates under a surprisingly dark and stormy-looking sky. So there are two triangles providing a light-dark contrast together with a horizontal cut-off in light and dark lines.

The rhythm comes from the stark lines of the terraces and the houses of the city. Finally, the

interchange between lit and unlit surfaces gives the picture a further contrast, this time between cold and warm areas. A good example of those two ingredients of every successful photograph: a trained eye . . . . and a certain amount of luck!

PLANTATION BY THE RIVERBANK

The motivation for this photograph came from the barely visible white plastic strips that are wound around the bottom of the stakes in this plantation. Fortunately there are also other elements which produce the attractive result we see here: a clear parallelism and an intriguing quality contrast in the lowest and highest parts of the image – dark-brown stakes against a light-brown background and bright green trees against the brownish-green water. Even then, the picture would not have a great deal of interest were it not

for the subtle 'white' lines running along the rows of stakes.

A special factor in the composition is the patch of white blossom in the trees along the water's edge. Here, lighting played an important part because the sunlight had nullified the quality contrast. Also, the camera position was chosen to produce a distinct assymetric effect, thereby avoiding the danger of triviality.

MONOCHROME

The main feature of this winter landscape is the use of monochrome to achieve a particular atmospheric effect. At the same time, however, we must not ignore the extent to which the composition is built up through a careful choice of camera position.

The foreshortened roadway divides the picture vertically into two almost exact halves, but disappears at almost the precise point where the diagonals cross, thereby producing a horizontal axis in the image.

At the right, there is a relatively large and light-coloured group of trees, held in balance by the smaller but darker group at the left. In much the same way, the clear white triangle of roadway in the foreground is offset by the smaller triangles formed by the roofs in the background.

However, the most important element of all is undoubtedly the figure of the woman walking along the road. It is not just that she acts as an indication of scale, or even as a point of interest in an otherwise dead landscape, important though both these factors are in themselves. Her main function is to bring something alive, something human into the picture and something warm into the midst of all that cold greyness. In this way, the picture becomes a story; it has something to tell and this heightens the expression considerably.

This in turn leads to the consideration of yet another pair of contrasting elements – landscape and man. When you think about it, you realise that it is a sort of form-contrast, such as long/short, large/small, sharp/blunt, etc: Yet at the same time there is a distinct difference between the effect, say, of a small plant in among a vast mountain landscape and a similarly small human figure in the same context. Perhaps it has something to do with identification or of seeing ourselves there.

An industrial landscape, taken in 6 × 6cm format with a telephoto lens. The foreshortening effect is very impressive here, making the houses appear completely overshadowed by the factory.

One final point about this photo is worth noting – it was taken with a perfectly ordinary short-focus lens.

A different example of the use of monochrome is the photograph of trees shown on p. 18. It is at the same time an example of parallelism, yet a parallelism that is modified by the rhythmic patterns of the frost among the branches. It is indeed an extreme example of the limitation of working with colour, made possible first of all by the choice of subject and by the viewpoint that includes no foreground and no horizon to indicate scale.

If we look at it analytically, we see that it consists of three vertical groups. Moving from left to right, we see first of all a number of trunks that stand well clear of one another, followed by one single, clear-cut trunk near the centre and, finally, a very tightly-packed group near the right-hand edge of the picture. These three groups are separated by two relatively empty areas and, although the division of surfaces they produce is not obvious, at first glance, it is nevertheless extremely important to the overall photographic composition.

FORM, LINE AND FORMAT

There's no question about the format of this photograph – it is absolutely dictated by the subject, a strong rectangular shape with firm intersecting perpendiculars. At the same time, the innate harshness of the subject is relieved by the hanging greenery and the uneven widths of the railing timbers; while the row of pots both accentuates and interrupts the basic rectangle. In other words, the pots, railing and plants provide a vertical element in the composition.

The summery atmosphere of this verandah is provided by the indirect lighting reflected from the frontage opposite and from the unreal colours that result from this shimmering light-effect.

Compared to the winter scene in the photograph on p. 75, the man in this picture is of little importance. He is a sort of 'prop', confirming what the photograph has already told you. However, he helps with the suggestion of the concept 'house', assisted by the protecting screen of hanging plants and the small details that show this as a place where someone lives.

CHANGE OF CAMERA POSITION

Sometimes the most attractive subjects provide the greatest problems. This village in southern Italy was a case in point. At first sight, it was fascinating, but it was far from easy to find a camera position that brought out the essential character of it.

Both the photographs shown here were taken with a 135mm lens, but the first was taken from a fairly high vantage-point and ended up looking as unimpressive as any holiday postcard. Not even the strong diagonal, so often praised as a design element, can help in this case. The slopes to left and right look too low and the uppermost houses merge indistinctly with the skyline.

A scramble down into the valley was necessary in order to find a lower camera position, and the second photograph is the result. Now there is tension in the way the town tumbles down from the heights. The building at the top right is caught in the middle of a powerful movement by the left-leading angle below, which in turn is balanced by the right-leading angle above. The centre of the picture is now no longer at a point where the diagonals cross, but somewhat to the right of it. Again, the lower slopes at the left are much more interesting because of the lower

camera-position and they add considerably to the balance of the composition.

The small area of white formed by the stable hewn out of the rock and the repetition of the same shape in the background colour is also of significance. Most important of all is the way in which the town is now outlined against the sky which, it should be noted, has been made to look darker by underexposing one and a half stops.

This under-exposure has not only made the sky look darker but also increased the tension in the photograph. This is important because the fascination of this subject lies in the fact that the town grows like a plant in the cleft between the two hills, springing up from the root of the cliff. The colour situation, in frontal lighting, gave only a little colour contrast to the subject and the rose-tinted roofing tiles have come out looking almost exactly the same colour as the dun rocks all around. They in turn have gained a little relief through the sparse growth of trees on the lower slopes. So, in this subject, increase in colour and form content means an increase in expression. Underexposure, therefore, is often an essential tool in creating a successful composition.

virtuous time waiting until the whole view was entirely clouded over and therefore evenly lit. So now we have the second picture in which, although there is less straightforward contrast, there is a much better relationship between the white of the houses and the green of the landscape. Also, by moving the camera to the left and to a slightly higher position, the white buildings in the foreground are put into a better position vis-a-vis the other buildings in the picture and their repetition adds to the rhythm of the composition. These buildings, incidentally, are called 'trulli', and are round houses with conical roofs typically found in the region of Albarabella, in Italy.

BACKLIGHTING

In the photograph of reeds and water, the potential of backlighting has been exploited to the full. The atmospheric effect obtained from the rows of reeds is superimposed on the central compositional element of a triangle with its base at the bottom of the picture and this adds stability and direction. The emphasis on horizontals gives a certain amount of restfulness and brings a rhythmic balance to these diverse elements.

From a compositional point of view, the right-leaning heads of the reeds, and the repetition of this effect in the background are very significant. Even more significant is the way in which the picture is divided into 'planes' by the light-surfaces. Despite the rhythmic pattern provided by the reeds, the picture would be chaotic without this division.

It is also important to remember that the light-conditions in situations like this last for only a very little while. You have to wait for them and then react when they occur. In this case, the light would have moved off to the right and the effect would have been lost. It is no accident that the shadow areas in this photograph are finely detailed; density is a function of lighting, and the lighting was carefully chosen with this in mind. Other factors that had to be taken into account are the illuminating effect of the mist, the relative thinness of the reed-heads and the fairly long exposure required. Exposure couldn't be altered too much because changes in aperture had to be kept to a minimum. Also, a lens-hood was essential since reflections would have spoiled the effect completely.

While the graphic elements are important, the contrasts are perhaps even more important in the overall effect produced by this picture. In particular, there is the cold-warm contrast of the

Both photographs shown here were taken from more or less the same position, except that, in the second, the camera had been moved a little to the left. Between the times they were taken, the lighting had changed dramatically. In the first picture the foreground is overshadowed while the rest of the scene lies in bright sunlight giving an extreme light-dark contrast. This means that much detail is lost in the foreground, while the middle part of the picture is far too light. Not only this, but the landscape is divided by this lighting effect into two unrelated halves. It is therefore not one landscape but two, and two that have no connection with one another.

Patience, they say, is a virtue. Well, I had a

colours, which is lightly underscored by the not-so-noticeable light-dark contrast. Harsh contrast is definitely not wanted in this type of subject, so an optimum rather than a maximum level has been sought.

In fact, there is a mediator between these two forms of contrast—the polarity of the image. There is also yet another form of contrast present, the so-called geometric perception which is in fact a contrast between things nearby and things in the distance. However, this is in part a function of the light/dark contrast and, in this respect, it is worth quoting at length from Johannes Itten's book *Art and Colour* :

'Lightness and darkness, brightness and dimness, are of the most fundamental and crucial importance to human life and indeed to the whole of nature.

The colours black and white are the strongest means of expression for the painter. They are the ultimate extremes of a scale of perception, within which lie the whole range of grey tones, and all the colours. The inter-related problems of lightness and darkness of the pure colours must therefore be thoroughly understood because they are of fundamental importance to every created image. A painting can in general be made up of two, three or four areas of primary tones. The artist speaks of two, three or four "planes" which must relate fully to the main groups. There can be small variations of tone within each plane, but they must not be such as to interfere with the distinction between the main groups. It can be seen therefore that similarity of tone values is important to the maintenance of this principle and, if these planes or groups of main tones are not present, the composition loses all sense of order, clarity, and attraction.

It is the need to produce a sense of depth on a flat surface that requires the painter to work in such a series of planes. Within the planes themselves all unwanted depth effects can be eliminated, and this is done through the tone values used in each plane. In general, the planes used are those of the foreground, the middle ground and the background, but of course there is no need to have the main figures of the painting in the foreground. It is often useful to have the fore-

ground lying between the viewer and the main subject, located somewhere in the central plane of the painting.

The use of a small range of colours is characteristic of all composition that are based upon lightness-darkness contrast. Since this type of contrast has a strong plastic effect and therefore alters spatial relationships, the painter must foresee all such possibilities with the greatest precision. One of the means at his disposal is the elimination of elements producing a plastic effect in adjacent image planes.'

. . . and you don't really have to substitute the word 'photographer' for 'painter' in this quotation to learn its lessons!

FRONTAL LIGHTING

Most people will tell you that frontal lighting is to be avoided and, generally, they are right. Direct light falling on a subject from the front makes it look flat and uninteresting and it also makes colours look garish and cheap. You know the sort of thing–the girl-friend, in a bright red dress, sitting on a green lawn in brilliant sunlight which makes her look as if she's sitting in a bowl of green pea soup, or the rich landscape photographed for its colour but without regard for form, composition, content or feeling.

So, if you want to avoid this sort of thing and if you want your photographs to be more than snapshots, you should take the conventional advice and keep away from frontally-lit subjects.

page 82/83.
A rather 'lived-in' rock-face! This was taken in between heavy rain showers using a 50mm lens. Much of the effect is obtained through concentration on the subject created by the compositional element of empty corner areas.

But, like all rules, this too has its exceptions. There are some motives that actually benefit from frontal lighting; only a few, but they do exist.

The photograph on the right is an example. Here, the frontal lighting is an essential element in the composition. As ever, it is the subject which dictates the treatment; a bright green meadow would never have stood up to this approach. It is the combination of the trained eye plus experience with the camera that sees the possibilities and uses them.

What are the possibilities? First of all, there is an image which is monochrome in the sense that it is made up chiefly of a single colour. This colour, hard to define, lies between brown and yellow (bolder than brown and quieter than yellow) and dominates that whole subject-area. And although this colour-dominance arises as a result of the theme, it is in itself inadequate as an expression of the theme. So something else has to happen in the picture.

There is a certain amount of natural interest arising from the push to the right supplied by the motion of the plant-heads, but this is still not enough. We therefore have to make something happen, and this is done by creating zones of sharpness and unsharpness through the deliberate use of aperture and depth-of-field effects (differential focus).

This is the second important point about this example. We are creating the image planes mentioned in the last section. There is the unsharp foreground which separates the image from the material, making it abstract; then there is the sharp intermediate plane against which the strip of blue provides a complementary contrast before passing on to the vague and unsharp background. Blue is often a restful colour, but not here because, although they lie in the zone of unsharpness, the brilliant flecks of colour from the surface of the restless water provide their own tension. There is a similar tension in the unsharp foreground zone just below the centre.

In order to produce the right sort of result from this material, a long-focus lens was necessary. I therefore used a 135mm telephoto, and of course had to take extreme care over my aperture setting.

LIGHTING CONTRAST

The two previous examples are of a contemplative, almost academic, nature. They require a clear insight into what you can and what you cannot do, as opposed to what you are trying to do, and you can almost see the finished photo before you take it.

If on the other hand you go out into the wilds, the process is entirely different and much more adventurous. For equipment, you certainly need a really long telephoto, such as a Telyt 400 and, with it, a good stable tripod. With this setup, you can get good close-ups of wild animals in a safari-park without putting yourself in danger. Or you can use it in a zoo to shoot through the bars or netting which separate you from the animals, making them look as if they are free.

You can also go into the real world of nature and photograph non-dangerous animals, even domestic animals, with impressive results. But you have no time for the careful selection of these subjects and no time for arranging compositional elements. Just looking and waiting and, when a subject presents itself, shooting. And shooting, shooting and shooting again! You have to fire off as many frames as you can while the chance

exists. Not for nothing are wildlife photographers called film-gobblers!

The results, however, can be very rewarding, as this example shows. It was out in the countryside of the Cevennes, in France, that a flock of sheep suddenly appeared in the viewfinder. As the depth-of-field of a telephoto is much less than that of a standard lens, you have to be that much more accurate with your focusing. At the same time, you are selecting the aperture, and this affects the depth of field. It's all happening and you've no time for indecision. This is where your training comes in because you should be doing these things without thinking, allowing your mind to concentrate on the scene as it appears in the view-finder, so as to capture the atmosphere and the story before it is gone.

Much later, when the film is developed, you will find out whether you were successful. You look

at your series of photographs, evaluating them with a view to choosing the right one. And that is an art in itself. You have to identify all the essential compositional elements and decide where they clash and where they mesh before you finally select one to print.

Of the range of shots I took of the sheep in the Cevennes, I chose the one on the previous page for three reasons: (1) the strong light-and-shade effect; (2) the cold-warm contrast; (3) the diagonal path of the sheep which, along with the attractive accents of the silhouetted trees, gives a fine suggestion of space. Without the harsh white outlines given to each sheep this photo would not be worth printing. With them, there is a dramatic black-white contrast that produces an almost stereoscopic effect.

Also, the cold-warm contrast emphasises the activity of the image, while the zones of unsharpness in the foreground and background generate a more gentle atmosphere that offsets the harshness of the blacks and whites, giving the picture that little something extra that makes it worthwhile.

WAITING FOR THE LIGHT

Shot in the French Alps, this is the sort of subject no photographer could ignore – a most interesting group of trees seen at about noon on a fine day in early spring. There was no problem about where to shoot from and it was clear that a 135mm lens would produce exactly the result I wanted. But it was equally clear that the lighting was quite wrong and that the sun on the white wall of the mountain in the background would overwhelm the photograph. However, just for comparison, I took one under those conditions: it is the one on the left, and you will see at once what I mean.

The photograph on the right was taken much later in the day, after the sun had moved away from the mountain. The cool evening light makes the image bluer and produces a more balanced composition. Despite the presence of mighty natural forces, the trees have a strangeness and

stillness about them, a presence of their own that they did not have in the earlier photograph. In that picture, their branches were lost against the bright background but now they stand out clearly as a network of fine white lines. Restrained use of colour has given the picture a unity it did not have before and the almost human forms of the trees are allowed to come into their own.

This example is an object lesson in the virtue of waiting for the light. But even more than that it is an example of a picture in which the type of lighting, the colour temperature and the structure and shape of the subject all came together to produce the desired composition. The optical distance from the visible reality is linked to the deliberate amplification of the attraction of the forms to give the subject its special bizarre, almost ghostly effect. It is also an exceptionally clear illustration of the naivety of ever photographing things 'as they are'.

COLOUR AND TIME

In the photograph on the left which is a view of the French town of Les Beaux, the mysterious colour effect is entirely a function of the atmospheric conditions. A moderately heavy rain shower had just passed over and was still hanging over the mountain in the background. At the same time, the setting sun suffused the valley with a deep red light. The raindrops reflected the red glow, thus producing in effect a backlit photograph.

Once again, an example of how colour is not an inherent property of things, but a product of the light.

So what colours may we expect to find in the light at various times of day? In the morning, it is almost yellow. If you look at the upper of the two photographs opposite with a trained eye (covering the lower one with your hand), it will be apparent that it was taken in the morning at around ten o'clock. This is shown by the colour of the roofs and the tops of the trees.

The light at midday is neutral white but it becomes more orange as the afternoon progresses, until an intense red is achieved at sunset. The picture opposite shows this very clearly. Once the sun is down, the light rapidly becomes blue in colour. The lower of the two pictures on this page was taken at the 'blue hour', although there was still enough colour left in the sky to add a slight reddish tint to it.

Once you get the idea of using the 'colours of time', as they might be called, you can apply them to your colour photography. And this, of course, is one area in which it differs very much from black-and-white.

COMPOSITION WITH COLOUR

When using these 'time colours' we have to take account, not only of the colour itself, but its interaction with the surroundings. The characteristic and effect of a colour is a function of its relationship with nearby colours. You have to get away from the sort of thinking used in black-and-white work:–

> *In pictorial composition, colour has an effect entirely different from the tone values and compositional factors in black-and-white work.*

The idea that the various grey tones occurring between deep black and bare white can be directly translated into colours is incorrect and leads to considerable misunderstanding. Two different colours photographed in black and white can produce exactly the same grey tone, whereas in a colour photograph they would interact through any of the mechanisms previously described. For every colour, there is a whole range of tones, and each of these has its own set of interactions with all the tones of every other colour. From a compositional point of view, therefore, colour is very much more complex than black and white.

This should be clear from an examination of the landscape overleaf. Had it been shot in black and white, the strong parallelism of the foreground, the roundness in the centre and the merging of shapes in the background would all have been recorded. Even the differences between the main colouration and that of the two yellow fields at the left and right of the middle background would have been apparent. But the cold/warm contrast between earth and sky which is such an essential element in the composition would have been utterly lost and the emotional content of the picture would have been much less.

Once again the 'colour of time', the orange-red of the late afternoon, has played a vital part.

Sunsets

ATMOSPHERIC SITUATIONS

Throughout the ages, the colours of sunset have been a constant source of pleasure to creative artist and casual observer alike. Not unnaturally, therefore, photographers have also been attracted to them. I'd imagine that if all the photos and slides of sunsets that have been taken since the advent of colour photography were piled up in one place, you'd need an oxygen mask to breathe at the top! Yet the sad truth is that, in the vast majority of cases, all these photographs have ended up as little more than pretty pictures.

Part of the trouble is that the sunset will not wait around for the photographer. In other words, the balance of light and colour changes so rapidly that, by the time the necessary measurements and adjustments have been made, the moment is gone and something different has taken its place. Also, there is the inevitable feeling that, because the sunset has exercised such an enchantment on mankind (not only mankind; there is evidence that some types of ape are also affected) and has been so often photographed and painted by very many different artists that there is nothing new to say about it. This couldn't be further from the truth. Each person sees each sunset in his own unique way as a completely new experience. Therefore, each person is in theory capable of reproducing this unique experience in the form of a colour photograph.

Of course, it is not only the colours of sunset that exercise such a unique and universal effect. It is the whole sense of atmospheric change with the onset of night, the sense of stillness and of confrontation with majestic nature that creates such a deep psychological impact. This of course can lead to over-romanticism and to sentimentality. Then the subject becomes taboo. But there are many much-photographed romantic subjects that are not taboo, so there is no reason why you should not photograph sunsets. What you should do is look for a completely different way of recording the fantastic possibilities presented by sunset colour-play; a way that is uniquely your own.

BEGINNING TO END

The conditions before sunset lend themselves to some interesting possibilities. You can shoot directly into the sun when it is quite a good way above the horizon, provided that its intensity has been reduced somewhat by cloud or mist and that you use a small aperture and short exposure (say f/22 at 1/250 sec). It is also important to use a

long-focus lens, otherwise the sun's disc will look too small in the picture.

On the other hand, the indirect approach, in which the horizon is kept high in the picture and only the reflection of the sun on the landscape is seen, can be very effective. The same applies to situations in which the sun is kept out of shot to the side, as in the photograph of Lake Balaton in Hungary on the previous page.

The examples were taken on a still summer evening when the colours simply begged to be photographed. The air was hazy and the whole of nature seemed to be wrapped up in itself.

I began with the sun still quite high. The first photo shows the light of the as-yet-unseen sun reflected in the main plane of the picture, while the middle and rear grounds fade to a dark Prussian blue near the edges of the print. The relationship between the foreground and the rest of the image area is such that a horizontal as well as a vertical format seems to be present. At the same time, the silhouetted outlines of the wooden frames and the lonely fisherman are very important, binding the horizontal and vertical elements together. A deliberate under-exposure makes sure that we retain an atmosphere of evening, perhaps even of night, in this picture.

In the second photograph, the horizon has been placed somewhat lower so that the sun can come into shot. Also, the camera position has been shifted a little to the left so that the human figure is centred in the zone of reflection. The brightness of the sun is tempered by the hazy atmosphere, and, at this stage of the sunset, it is still high enough to look full and round. Later, its image is deformed by the optical distortion of the thick layers of air it must penetrate when it is near the horizon.

In this photograph, symmetry is an important factor. It was just as important to place the sun in precisely the centre of the frame as it was to get the angler slightly out of centre. However, it is even more important to note the reddish colour of the reflection repeated in the slight halo visible around the disc of the sun.

In the third picture, taken after sunset from the same place, although now in horizontal format, the rows of horizontal lines produce a feeling of balance and restfulness. Also, the subtle colours of the 'blue hour' create an impression of unreality giving the photograph much of its impact. It is usually only possible to get a full series of photographs like this over water, where there is an uninterrupted view to the west. Or indeed to the east, for very much the same considerations apply to photographs of the sunrise as well.

Portraits

page 98/99.

Two portraits taken against different backgrounds—dark against dark, light against light. A little asymmetry is introduced into the first by allowing the vertical line of the boarding to cut the dark-coloured cap off-centre. In the second, it is very important to make sure that the white hair, whiskers and moustache show up lighter than the background. The second photograph is of a small gypsy camp, and is a deliberately posed shot, including the positioning of the metal pots. The diagonal placing of the subjects and the emphasis this gives to the hands are the main compositional factors in this photograph.

FRIENDLY REPORTAGE

We are not machines. The development of our individual personalities, together with the ways in which our lives have unfolded and the characteristics we have acquired, all affect the way we express ourselves. They affect the way we see things and the way we choose to communicate the things we see. Of course, I am no exception to this, and the painter I used to be is always standing by my side directing me, so that the result is often more design conscious than photographic.

I'm not saying that I think exclusively in terms of graphics. But I do think that in portraiture there is another dimension of interperson relationship, which is not present in other types of work. If you are photographing a landscape or a still-life, it is just a matter of you and the subject, how you see it and how you choose to express the impression it makes on you. When the subject is human, however, there is a world of difference. There is no longer just the question of how you feel, but also of how *he* feels.

You can always just point and shoot of course—just take snapshots and just use human beings as objects.

But if you really want to get the best out of photographing your fellow humans, you must establish this interchange with the subject. You may not want just to take a simple portrait; it is all to the good if you include your subject's environment, too. But even if you only see your work as reportage, it must always be friendly reportage.

JAN PUSS, THE PRIMITIVE

If you have a neighbour like Jan Puss, then you're very lucky indeed. When I took these photographs Jan was 82. He is built like a tree, has hands the colour and texture of wood and takes *size 12* shoes. Every day, from early morning to late in the evening, you will see him working in his garden or in the potting-shed and he has never had a day's illness in his long life. And his nickname? He earned the title 'puss' way back in childhood because he used to lick his plate!

Good neighbourliness was in fact the starting-point of this series of photographs. In the first one, he is sitting on his step, a home-made hoe across his knees, loosely held in his huge hands. He looks easily at the lens, soberly but not with any animosity. It is immediately clear that he has lived his life with dignity, that he is as he is and feels well on it. I used a 50mm lens for this and kept the picture sharp, not only on Jan himself but also on the immediate surroundings. There is a direct connection between the sober dignity of the old man and the straight lines of the wall, the age of the door behind him and the brickwork which surrounds it.

For the second photo on the previous page, I used a super-wide-angle lens. This produced a deliberate distortion of his hands and feet, emphasising their size and solidity; he found this most amusing when he saw the result! While taking the photos we talked idly about this and that, which of course sets up the relationship between photographer and model that we mentioned before, and avoids any self conscious poses. Despite the distortion of the lens, which in fact makes the surroundings somewhat less realistic, the man himself is absolutely authentic. The over-emphasis on the size of the hands and feet (helped by the fact that the hands are more open in this photo) which might otherwise be a little grotesque, is completely offset by that disarming smile.

In both pictures, the figure is kept out of the centre, thereby avoiding stiff symmetry while still allowing the maximum attention to be directed at the main subject.

The third example (left) in this series is a straight-forward portrait. The close proximity of the 50mm lens disturbed my model not in the least. I wanted to get this close with a standard lens to emphasise the nose and flatten the ears slightly, but there is still no sign of artificiality in the portrait. Old Jan looks back at the eye of the camera with a level, alert gaze, completely at ease. The last photo (below) in the series shows Jan at work. This was taken with a 135mm lens from quite a high position. We see him here in profile, both hands occupied in tying up the bean-plant with workman's hands, as in paintings by Millet. The picture is clearly more static than the other three, but in this way expresses the powerful personailty of Jan Puss, set with inalienable solidity in his natural workplace.

Before I leave Jan and his photos, I would just like to note that the light was again ideal: a bright day without sun, giving a soft indirect light which was just right for portrait work.

◄Portrait of a woman. There is a contrast between the clearly-lit face and the dark background while the direction in which she is looking intersects the diagonal made by the line of the head and the visible shoulder.

PORTRAIT OF A FRIEND

Surroundings are extremely important in portrait work – more so, perhaps, than in any other aspect of photography. They require careful treatment, and this can vary from keeping a coloured background out of focus to a deliberate attempt to create a particular environment.

This is illustrated by the two photographs above. A friend was repairing his roof and was making his way through the skylight. The first picture is less attractive: there is an unwanted assymmetry in the picture and the left-inclined body looks unnatural. The whole thing looks posed and artificial.

On the other hand, the second picture in which the model is taken frontally with his hands folded under his chin, and is looking straight at the camera is quite natural. He is set almost exactly at the centre of the picture, and all the lines of the roofing tiles now frame him quite accurately. This perspective effect gives the picture its strong characterisation.

Both photos were taken with the same 21mm wide-angle lens from a close viewpoint.

Children

PERSONALITY

The making of a good photograph of children is more difficult than it seems. Far too often we see the same old situations; the little girl with the roguish eyes at the telephone, the baby drinking his milk or, worst of all, the terribly stiff and unnatural school portrait. Some actual snapshots are interesting fortunately, but not very often. But it is quite literally the snapshot that is best for children. The capturing of the child in action, busy with the things in his hands and full of wonder or full of defiance, leaves the personality of the child intact and does not force it into the adult shape of whatever preconception may be in the photographer's mind.

And that is the secret of good child photography – leaving the personality intact. This means that you must have an empathy with your subjects, putting your own thoughts and ideas aside and having a total respect for, and agreement with, those of the children you are photographing. In other words, you must become a child yourself. This is the only way in which you will get a real child portrait; one that is original and not in the conventional mould.

From the point of view of sheer form, the two examples shown on these pages are not especially striking. The two little girls in the doorway of the caravan are certainly intent on posing with their dolls. But this was what they wanted to do; I did not direct them, they were just enjoying themselves. The one striking thing about this picture is the poster on the inside of the open door, which gives the picture just enough addity to make it interesting.

In the same way, the picture of the little girl with the big doll is very straightforward. Although the torso of the doll and the variety of the materials in the shot are of interest, the photo is still of necessity a portrait. A static photo, but it tells its story clearly. This little mother is ready to defend her baby against all comers and especially against the man with the camera! She is, therefore, in contact even though I was using a 135mm lens from some way off.

The soft lighting was a factor of considerable advantage in this photograph. Also, the curve of the bottom of the doll's dress, which reflects the pattern in the plaster wall above the little girl's head, is quite important to the overall composition.

DEPTH-OF-FIELD EFFECTS

The first of the photographs on the left facing page, is an example of something the books say you should never do; it is a photograph taken from an adult eye level looking down at a child. It is not the sort of 'snapshot' I have been recommending to you because the scene was almost set up in a cemetary in the Dordogne on a warm summer midday, with the child (my own little daughter, in fact) resting her head against the edge of an old tombstone. I also have to admit that she was standing on her mother's back and that *she*, with great patience, was lying on the ground behind the tombstone!

The background was made up of grave ornaments such as plastic flowers and beads and the colour-mist effect was obtained by using a long-focus lens (400mm) with a wide-open aperture and a little bit of over-exposure. This made the background fade away despite the light coming from the rear, and it removed the distance effect which I did not want. The main technical problem that had to be overcome was the very precise focusing that was needed when using a 400mm lens to separate the little model from the background.

Then came the bonus, the one element I had not planned. My little model, lulled by the warmth of the afternoon, closed her eyes and let her head droop on her arms. Her whole manner became, quite naturally, completely expressive of childhood, innocent, trusting and asleep. The photograph, of course, gained a whole new significance – a poetic element, a childhood dream.

The second example on this page is nowhere near so complex. It is a pure snapshot, a spontaneous photograph taken by a lucky photographer swinging his camera round almost at random in a gypsy camp.

Going back to the use of depth-of-field effects, however, it must be noted that there is a design decision to be made when using it. You have to make up your mind which part of the subject needs to be sharp to get the maximum interest into the picture, and then concentrate on it. The rule is, look, choose and concentrate.

This is expressed very well in these two photographs of the child and her soap-bubbles. The first impulse is to concentrate on the girl and not on the bubbles, which just float past the model as a sort of prop. However, on a more searching look at what is presented in the viewfinder, a new possibility reveals itself – concentrate on the bubbles.

Experience makes this sort of realisation second

nature. You are immediately aware that, even though she is out of focus, the child is still the prime source of interest in the photograph. Set against the dark background, she provides the balance the picture needs in the position she takes relative to the rest of the composition. The viewer's attention is rivetted on this essential piece of action – the soap-bubble set against the open mouth which expresses so well the desire and attention of the child.

To get this sort of photograph you must not be miserly with film and you should shoot off as many frames as you can while the moment exists. In this one, everything has worked out just right – the soap bubble right next to the expressive mouth, the balance of position and colour, and the diagonal formed through the line of the three in-focus bubbles leading the eye from bottom left to top right.

Although there is an inevitable element of luck in child photography, it is experience that makes sure of getting something worthwhile. The early training enables you to balance up a photograph and to look for lines, textures and colours without thinking about it. This is exactly how the first of

these two photos came to be. With wide-open aperture, I focused on the bubble and the rest took care of itself.

Focusing on the child produces a photograph like the one in the second example. Here, a change of camera position has brought the flowers into a different position, thereby producing a wholly different effect. Now we see all of the upper part of the child's body and the movement implied by the positions of the hands, arms and shoulders. The depth of field has been greatly increased here through the use of a smaller aperture, so that the soap-bubbles are sharp, as well as the child herself. The inclination towards the left of the child's body is just offset by the movement to the right of the bubbles as they blow away in the breeze.

These are really two contrasting styles in photography. The first is poetry in which expression is more important than content, whereas the second is much more anecdotal. It does not however totally lack poetry – no good story ever does.

Just a word on lighting to finish – take your exposure measurements on the light areas so that the shadows come out darker.

PORTRAIT WITH STILL-LIFE

In this photograph (right), there can be no doubt that the expression on the face of the child is a major factor in the picture's overall effect. All the careful arrangement that went into it would not have counted for much had it not been for the pensive, faraway look in the eyes of the little girl when the photograph was actually taken. It becomes an expressive portrait study which, despite the child's inwardness, still shows a strong link between herself and the photographer who was in fact her father! The physical barrier that separated us – the glass of the window through which she was peeping – was no problem; with the sort of contact we had, a simple gesture was enough to indicate what was wanted.

As far as the content of such pictures is concerned, the photographer finds himself torn between two opposing requirements: on the one hand the realisation of a given compositional idea and, on the other, the expression of the personality of the child in its own world of fantasy. It is indeed difficult to walk the knife-edge between creative intuition and technical detachment.

To avoid any falseness, I used only the available daylight because I wanted no reflections of artificial lighting in the picture. The composition is therefore characterised by great pale colours, supported by the clear bottom-left to top-right diagonal.

The sort of contact we need between child-model and photographer can only come about if there is also a strong element of trust present. For this reason, the child should be used to the camera, and regard it as an everyday object, although this might not be easy in some cases. It should nevertheless still be possible even for the spare-time photographer to build up enough trust with the children he wants to capture on film. Once the child realises what is wanted – perhaps even has a look through the viewfinder himself – he can become his own director. A couple of hours invested in play like this can produce a return in terms of results far in excess of anything you might have expected.

BACKLIGHTING

Strong backlighting need not just produce silhouettes. It is always possible to use curtains and shutter to reflect light at the subject and fill in the shadowed areas. This is especially true with lace or muslin curtains which diffuse light and give a pleasing effect, what the professional calls 'diffused reflection'. However, there is always a considerable amount of difficulty involved in light measurement under such conditions and if you just guess at the exposure you are almost certain to be wrong.

It is very important – and especially so with slides – that the lightest parts of the picture are not bleached out. You take your light measurement therefore on the lightest part of the subject i.e the white curtains. To be on the safe side, use a lens hood to keep out reflections. The photograph overleaf was taken with a hand-held camera using a 50mm lens at f/5.6.

It is not advisable to use fill-in flash for these situations. Although it will certainly lighten the deepest shadows, it can utterly destroy the delicate colouring which is an essential feature of the composition.

Here, we come back to the main point of this whole book; the use of colour as a design element in photography and the development of creative vision as a basic tool for achieving this. Reality consists not only of external forms. There are

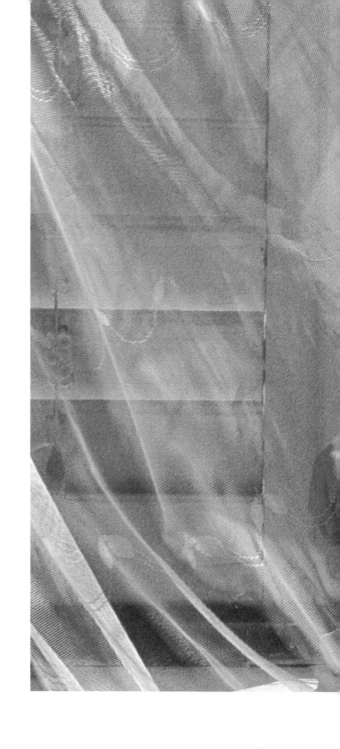

other aspects to the reality of a thing that have to be brought out, and this can only be done, paradoxically, by removing oneself from the apparent reality (superficially is perhaps a better word) and looking beyond it into what is usually termed the abstract.

FAST-ACTION SHOTS

A genius such as Cartier-Bresson, who seems to see movement and action before it happens, is rare indeed. We lesser mortals usually find it extremely difficult to take good 'snapshots', and here I mean photographs in which the action is 'snapped' in an instant of time; not holiday pretties! We need a good deal of luck and that is a matter beyond our control. For this reason, then, you should expect a lot more misses than hits in this game—a hundred to one is not too bad a score!

A certain amount of 'direction' is therefore needed; not enough to lead to an unnatural-looking photo but enough to improve the odds a little. This is what we were doing with our child model at the fairground; by allowing her to play and enjoy herself we were 'directing' her, while at the same time looking for the action shot that was going to look and feel spontaneous afterwards.

Many adults feel a little unsure when they take a camera and try to capture the essence of a child at play, And, of course, the child knows this at once! He immediately begins to be curious, naughty, stubborn or shy. Even the best of these, curiosity, doesn't help the photographer because now the child knows something is watching him and wants to know what it is all about. It's no use telling him to 'do something'; this will only produce some awkward, unnatural-looking movement that will be no use at all. Even an adult cannot produce natural-looking facial expressions and body movements to order.

To get truly lifelike action photographs, it is necessary to choose the moment when the total personality of the model appears in its natural environment. So how do we achieve this? How do we solve the problems we have been discussing? First, make sure that the action is what the child wants to do itself and is not something imposed upon it from outside. The photographer should be as nearly absent as possible, busy with his own things and unobtrusive. At the same time, he must be always on the alert and sensitive to the child itself. What you can do with one child you cannot with another.

Young children are usually unselfconscious and are easily diverted; their play is much more important than some old guy with a camera. Older children, however, know what's going on and tend to show off when the camera is pointed at them. With them, you have to try looking elsewhere, while still keeping an eye on the child and waiting for the right moment to shoot. In these cases, anything resembling overt direction

is out. What you have to do is to manipulate the situation so that the child ends up doing what you want without realising it.

The children in these photographs were still at the unselfconscious stage. The little gypsy couple in the picture below were only a little bit surprised to see the photographer. The little girl looks questioning but hasn't a trace of fear or shyness about her, and the little fellow on the right is all for a closer acquaintance.

The two photographs of the little girl on the carousel are quite different. In the first one, she is totally engrossed in riding the horse and is quite unaware of the photographer. Her whole attitude expresses the wish to get on with things, for the carousel to start and for her steed to gallop away.

In the second photo, she is looking right at the camera, not in any way acting but simply showing her enjoyment to me when I called out to her. 'Isn't it great!', she seems to be saying and you can nearly hear the laughter, which is what I find most pleasing of all about this photograph.

I used a 135mm telephoto for both the carousel pictures. The narrow angle of view gives a tightness to the composition and there is a further advantage in the favourable perspective effect. The telephoto allows you to edit out elements in the photograph you don't want to include. Compositionally, the first photograph is satisfactory but there is far too much detail to distract the eye from the relationship between the child and the horse. For this reason, there is less tension in the picture than there might be; the horizontal format, with its more restful connotations is also partly responsible for this.

Just the opposite is the case in the other photo: the vertical format accentuates the action and unwanted visual distractions are kept out of shot. Child and horse are both rearing up in the same way and even the horse seems to be laughing. The arch in the background is now integrated into the composition, and the way it is left open at the right-hand side of the picture seems to invite the child and her horse to gallop away into the distance.

SOME GUIDELINES FOR SNAPSHOTS

Some readers may already be bored with this subject and, if so, I'm sorry. However, the main point of this section is to help those who really want to know all about the subject and, although the technique of action photography does not really come within the scope of a book on composition, it is still possible to lay down a few brief guidelines.

And a few guidelines is about all we can expect, for there can hardly be any rules for anything as ephemeral as capturing an instant in time. So what can we say; the action snapshot must be true to life. Well, yes. It could hardly be otherwise! What else? It must be a photographic masterpiece; it must be compositionally and technically perfect. Yes again. But if we are going to go on like this we will either be continually stating the obvious or else limiting the field of action until all possibility of spontaneity is lost.

This is why I say guidelines rather than rules. What I say below is meant to be used as a guide only and to be ignored as soon as the moment calls for it. If all the above rules were to be strictly observed, the photo at the right would never have got into print!

So now we come to the 'rules' themselves

1. Keep your eyes open and don't spare your film. The most interesting events happen by chance and without warning.
2. So far as possible, try to be where the action is. You may not be able to forecast that something interesting will happen, but you can certainly guess where it won't!
3. Keep your camera at the ready.

THE FAIRGROUND

The colour impression given in the picture opposite by the light falling on the points of major interest is undoubtedly an important compositional element; the delicate grey-blue of the shadows providing an emphasis for the golden morning light shining on the main subject. This may seem an unimportant detail, but in the picture as a whole it is critical. Even in this modern age of photography, the principle discovered by the old masters that weak colours can interact to produce strong effect still holds.

In this photograph, there is of course a quantity contrast (much against little) but there is also light and dark contrast. Due to the intensity of the sidelighting, the shadows look darker than they actually are; in fact, if you cover over the light parts you will see that they are not really dark at all. This effect provides clarity, calling attention to the central subject in no uncertain terms.

In photographs like this, it is important to resist the temptation to freeze the action. It is just the *unsharpness* due to movement that gives the picture its active element and tones down the excessive detail. As a general rule, I would recommend working on a relatively long exposure of about 1/60 or even 1/30 sec, and taking the exposure measurement on the lightest detail. The effect produced is to regard the gondola as a

world within a world, and to make the child's fellow passengers pale and ghostlike.

I have to admit, however, that the pin-sharp image of the child owes something to luck. This type of fairground ride has of course two motions –the rotation of the gondola about the centre of the carousel, and the secondary rotation about its own centre. Taken together, they have a dead point, an instant at which part of the gondola stops in relation to other elements, and the child just happened to be at this point as the camera panned over her.

If you look through the photographic literature of bygone days, you will find paragraphs that read like this:–

'Anybody walking through fairground, playgrounds or sporting areas with his eyes open will find a wealth of suitable subjects for the camera. Nevertheless, with such subjects, he will have to choose his position and await his moment with great care . . . .'

They had real problems in those days! Today, with our superfast lenses and films, taking good snapshots should be easier than ever. So why don't we see them more often?

Why does the snapshot, the moment out of time, seem condemned to remain the province of a tiny minority, even in the future? Perhaps it is, as Heinrich Böll suggested, '. . . . because the familiar appearance, the artificial pose and the respectable compositions of our photographic forebears somehow look more human than snapshots do?'

page 120/121.

Two little girls behind the window of a caravan. A certain amount of direction was used here: they were asked to jostle about to get a look through the window. The waving hand was the main factor in deciding the moment to shoot. Taken with a hand-held miniature camera, using a 50mm lens. The blue of the curtain is of course an essential factor here.

CHILDREN AND ANIMALS

We start with three pictures of my daughter with a newborn lamb. A well known subject and certainly one with a lot of potential charm. Why can't we be traditional for once?

The first photo was taken in bright sunshine. The colour temperature was therefore relatively low, and the shadows were almost black. The expression on the face of the child and the position of her hands on the head of the lamb are the only good things about this picture!

The second example is rather better. The sun has now gone behind the clouds and the colours are in better balance because of the lighter shadows. But it is still not right. The child's head and that of the sheep do not make a harmonious pattern, and the sheep doesn't look very interested.

We have to give first prize to the third picture.

The gentle appearance of the hands and face of the child is now at its most apparent and the mother sheep has become a part of the composition. Again, no overt direction or planning. Just watching and waiting, and a little bit of luck on our side!

I have to admit that we don't always have sheep for our children to play with while we photograph them. More often, it's just the common old cat or dog. But that shouldn's matter in the least. It is still possible to get appealing and moving photographs like the upper illustration opposite. The love of the little girl for her pet is clearly and unsentimentally shown in what is literally a snapshot; a photograph taken when the moment was exactly right. The surroundings, the doorway and the step, help the overall composition but they also provide an everyday atmosphere to this photograph.

CHILDREN AND THEIR SURROUNDINGS

You will notice that I keep making rules and then breaking them! I've often railed against too much colour in a photograph and here is a picture that I think is an excellent example of child photography and it is positively bursting with bright colours!

But there must be no taboos in art. Rules are made to be broken, so they say, and these two little ones were almost begging to be photographed. In fact, the very intensity of the blue in the background is almost exactly matched by the blue of the first little girl's stockings while the flower patterns on the gate behind them, which look rather like angel's wings, combine with it to make an appealing photograph.

The three little ruffians in the upper of the two photographs opposite were potential film stars! I first tried a group (looking as if they'd just won the World Cup) set a little to the left in a horizontal format. But this cut off the rather interesting orange curve on the wall above them, so I tried again in vertical format. The result is I think an improvement. The paint streak now occupies the centre of the image area, but the eye is rapidly led downwards to the figure of the youngster squatting at the bottom left. He in fact acts as an indicator of scale by leading the eye back to the colour field, which now looks much more impressive in context.

FOR THE FAMILY ALBUM

How do you photograph your own children? As naturally as possible! Take a couple of kids, pull a couple of funny faces, wait for the right moment and press the shutter release. These two little fellows are as mischievous as they come, you just have to give them a chance to show off and they'll do the rest. It was a fortunate coincidence that the red in the jacket of the first child was reflected almost exactly in the colour of the other's boots.

Red and green provide a complementary contrast and the other important compositional element is the way in which these two little devils are set in the middle of the pathway so the perspective effect comes into play. Thus we get an unpretentious but balanced picture. Not a great example of photographic art, perhaps, but certainly a good one for the family album.

GROUPS

The starting point for the photographs (opposite) was the atmosphere of melancholy that surrounded these children and their tumbledown home in Jugoslavia, a situation that had to be used to optimum effect. The danger was, however, that the harsh poverty in which these children live would be over emphasised, and that would be no good at all.

The upper photograph shows the scene as I first saw it. The second one was obtained through deliberate direction. The scene is now limited to part of a wall and door of the hut. The environment in which the children live is now less explicit but in some ways clearer. The aim was to express the solemn solidarity of the children.

The central figure is the little girl with the tragic face, standing slightly to the left of centre. The two outer children, with their bodies and faces turned towards the centre, hold the group together. The tiniest one, with her puzzled face, provides a touching contrast to the sadness of her older sister both in terms of her size as well as in her facial expression.

The fact that the eyes of the two boys on the right look crossed and that the whites are clearly visible is a very important element in this composition. Because the group is placed in the shade the colours are cool and subdued, although there are a couple of touches of warm tone here and there to provide a little colour contrast. The whole picture is a gripping and moving story of children who have grown into adults before their time.

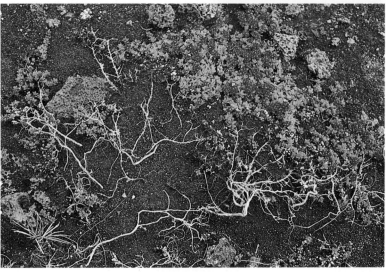

Still Life

WHAT STILL LIFE IS ABOUT

Briefly, still life can be defined as the representation of artistically arranged immobile objects. It's an odd sort of term because most of the things represented, although still, are not 'living' in any sense of the word. The French have a better term – *nature morte*, or dead nature – which seems to express rather better what this art form is about; but we had better keep to the term in use. Anything that has to do with mankind in any way, or which is part of nature, can be used as a still-

life subject. The many marks that man leaves behind him can certainly be used to good effect. In general, however, still-life subjects fall into two fairly distinct classes; chance subjects or things discovered fortuitously, and arranged subjects with things deliberately composed into an artistic array.

Chance still-life subjects are all around you. All you have to do is keep your eyes open. In the kitchen, the garden, the street and the churchyard—all sorts and kinds of subject present themselves in all sorts of places. Just try looking down, especially when you're walking along the beach. Among the shells at the waterline, you'll find all sorts of things—bits of wood, old shoes, bottles and even plastic rubbish, all set against the backdrop of the intricate patterns that water engraves on sand. You can take photos all day, lying flat on the sand or standing right above the subjects and looking down on them.

There is no inflexible rule that says you can't make alterations to these chance subjects if you want to. Depending on circumstances, you may want to move something, add something or take something away; after all it is your own compositional sense that counts. This is the grey area between chance and arrangement, but there is no virtue in sticking rigidly to one or the other. With completely arranged subjects, of course, the total concept is your own. The subject is built up from a series of individual items, an arrangement of objects made with the intention of creating a particular effect or perhaps something resembling an illusion. This makes special demands on your sense of composition, and your choice of components and arrangements will depend on your own vision and the relationship between the things you choose.

The two examples shown on the first page of this section are chance subjects. In both, there has been a deliberate attempt to obtain just the right section from a plane of interest, while the virtual monochrome of the subjects is also a factor in the composition. Chance, indeed, in the second example that the birds happened to perch there! A combination of still life and the snapshot!

FROST

An old door on a winter's morning and a spiderweb beaded with frost—a splendid still life subject. However, the grey morning light is rather too strong at the top right, causing an imbalance. If we take out the part around the bolt where the spiderweb is, the balance is much better. The harsh white horizontal line along the bottom of the door is no longer there to grab the eye and the bolt is now large enough to act as a focal point at the centre of the image. It connects aptly with the other important element, the web, which itself is balanced by the two smaller webs below. Two slanting crossbeams enclose the composition at the top, while the third one with the interesting pattern of white frost lines forms a counterweight to the upward movements of the bolt. These opposite movements are emphasised by the short horizontal line at the left.

GLASS AND ICE

Here we have an example of the other type of still life, the arranged composition. It was set up in front of a window and photographed from outside. The window-pane was covered with frost-flowers so that the objects are not themselves visible, but in fact make up a still-life silhouette. The source of the backlighting in this photograph was a pair of oil lamps set up on a table behind the subject and not too far away. A static subject, but one not without attraction.

However, this is certainly not just the result of the composition. The fine patterns of the frost-flowers, repeated in the delicate lines of the pea-cock feather, bind the composition together and are very important in creating the overall effect. The other factor which makes the picture attractive is the interesting variations of colour produced by reflections in the glass.

Because of the dim light, this photograph required a two-hour exposure. This in turn called for a good exposure meter, a solid tripod, a 135mm telephoto and an aperture of f/8. Also a pair of very cold feet!

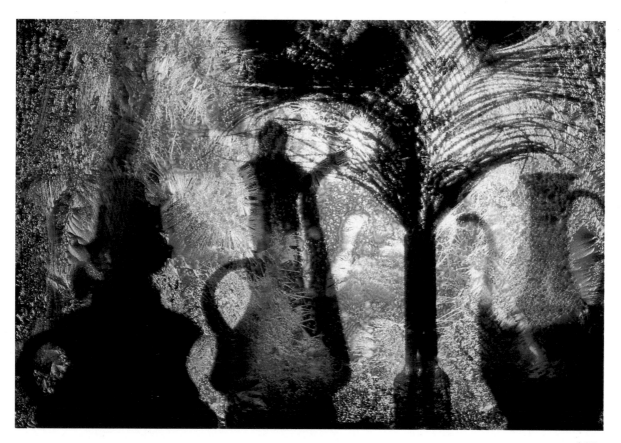

STILL LIFE WITH OIL LAMPS

This is more or less the reverse of the previous shot; the weather conditions weren't much different and the objects making up the composition had been changed, but it was taken from indoors by a warm fire, and that was certainly preferable! I was in my holiday cottage and it was early in the morning of a snowy winter's day.

The surreal atmosphere of this photograph hasn't much to do with the fact that the composition is made up of an arrangement of rather attractive antique objects. What is more important is the way in which the subject is used to combine a photographic with an aesthetic effect. It is not just a photo of oil lamps and old bottles; it is an attempt to communicate atmosphere, to tell a story and to bridge the gap between poetry and the commonplace.

Colour is of course vital; bright tones would have destroyed the effect utterly. Photographically speaking, much of the attraction lies in the interconnection of the objects and their surroundings; in this case the frozen window pane behind them. The suggestion of space behind the pane has been introduced by deliberately scraping clear a portion of the glass at the left, and making use of the other clear patch where the frost has melted at the right.

There has been no attempt, however, to create a poetic effect by the use of deliberate unsharpness. On the contrary, an almost over-serious approach has been taken.

Another factor in the composition is the way in which the heights and widths of the objects have been arranged and the balance created by the juxtaposition of colours. The most solid shapes and colours give the picture a firm base while the more interesting transparent items lie at the centre. Within the outer rectangular frame, the tops of the tallest lamp (at the left), the green bottle, and the centre of the bunch of garlic, form the apices of three notional triangles. The vertical window-frame, which would otherwise cut the picture in half, has been integrated by placing the blue-based lamp in front of it.

The photograph was taken using a tripod and a 135mm telephoto lens. A large sheet of white paper was laid on the floor in front of the window to provide fill-in lighting.

◄Window pane on a rainy day, taken from indoors using a 35mm camera with a 135mm lens at maximum aperture to get a shallow depth of field. The bizarre collection of plants in the background form a rich colour contrast with the paper cutout.

STILL LIFE WITH DEAD BIRD

Macabre realism and surrealism are held in balance in this picture. It is a horrific, but therefore interesting, theme! The dead bird, apparently the victim of some nocturnal predator lay on the tiles of my terrace.

Anyone wanting to use such a subject, in which content as well as form plays such a large part, must beware the danger of over-dramatisation. Without a careful compositional approach it can so easily degenerate into mere coarse decoration, sensationalising horror for its own sake.

In this case, the dead creature was carefully moved to the place in which it would provide the most effective composition, and the lines of the tile joints are an important factor in this. The wings and feet were spread out so that the bird intersects several surfaces. The tragedy is underscored by the way in which the foot lying on the borken tile is echoed by the pattern of the breakage. It is as if the dead bird is trying to escape from its broken surface.

Red and green form a complementary contrast which fulfils the inner purpose of this picture, showing raw reality yet hinting at a deeper significance.

Form,
Rhythm
and
Structure

WINTER LANDSCAPE WITH WINDMILLS

There are always problems with snowscapes, especially with overcast skies, because of the enormous variation in brightness contrast. Usually, the light reflected from the snow is about as bright as that of the sky itself.

In the above winter scene, which consists of many apparently unrelated elements, the silhouette effect is most striking. All these elements stand out equally against the stark white backdrop and thereby obtain a unity they would not otherwise have had. Form and colour also play an important part. Dark horizontal and vertical lines and sur-

faces are sharply defined against the lighter parts of the picture and the rhythmic effect of the foreground acts as a foundation for the whole composition.

The subtle reaction of the grey-green and grey-violet tones in this picture produces an unreality that would be lost in a black-and-white photograph. The overall effect is static, despite the rhythmic detail, largely because of the large areas of immaterial ground tone.

To get the best effect, a longer exposure than that indicated by the exposure meter was used in this photograph, and you can judge for yourself the excellent result obtained.

REFLECTIONS

The attraction of this subject lies in the rhythm and repetition of curving, moving lines, so that it is almost an abstract. In practice, it was high water on an absolutely still day after a very rainy period that made it possible.

The special effect lies in the balance between the almost identical images of the original reeds and their reflected images. This is not because there is any absolute symmetry between the halves; the observant reader will already have noticed that the reflections are about half as long again as the reeds themselves. Again, there is no clear dividing line between the upper and lower parts of the picture. If there had been, it would have divided the image into a pair of rectangles which, despite their apparent connection, would have lost the rhythmic movement which is the basis of this composition. For this reason I was careful to keep image and reflection to one continuous graphic unity extending over the whole surface of the photograph.

So this is not really a picture of reeds in the water, but a stress-field of rhythmic lines reminiscent of the images found in Japanese prints. There is a suggestion of the development of the forms, of how one moves relative to the other and how one is interwoven with the other. This is where the tension in the image comes from.

Despite the graphic strength and stability of the image, each line in the composition is flowing and leading the eye from detail to detail. The central point of this motion lies on the main axis slightly to the left and forms the starting point for the whole composition. Without this point, there would be no stability in the image at all. The deliberate cut-off at the right, and the similar one at the left, are essential to the continuing rhythm of the picture because they imply an infinite repetition of the swirling motion within the image format.

This was no lucky snap. A great deal of observation and weighing of compositional factors went into it in order to produce an optimum image. In cases like this, there is only one solution to the compositional problems which it sets, only one photograph that will do. It is usually necessary, however, to make several different exposures to ensure that everything is absolutely right.

ON THE NATURE TRAIL

In this dramatic nature photograph taken in Scotland, the most important form elements are to be found in stark trees lying under the stormy sky in the mid-plane of the picture. What little light there is seems to be centred on these skeletal trees, giving them a sinister plasticity. It is clear that storms always come from the left side of the picture, driving the trees into a permanent hunched posture as they lean away from the directional winds. So these naked trunks, starkly visible against the dark background, create a parallelism leading the eye away towards the right. The fact that such light as there is comes from the right, adds to this emphasis.

There are two clear basic curves in this picture; a line through the trees starting at the bottom right and leaving the picture at the left, and the line of the hills which repeat the form in the opposite direction. In fact they just about enclose the main part of the subject. The bright patch at the top right is repeated in the trunk of the tree which lies almost exactly at the point of intersection of diagonals. By contrast, it draws the eye to the merciless force of the storm, which is just entering the picture from the left.

RHYTHM AND PARALLELISM AGAIN

The related concepts of rhythm and parallelism have already been discussed at the beginning of this book and we have agreed that 'rhythm', the regular repetition of structures within a subject, creates many interesting opportunities in colour photography.

We have already looked at the composition 'Plus and Minus' of Piet Mondriaan (see page 38), so now let us compare it with the photograph 'Reeds and Water', taken in Norway during 1970 and reproduced overleaf. It was taken early in the morning when little waves were coming ashore in an unbroken progression. As we can see, Mondriaan's abstract structure of horizontal and vertical lines has its parallel in this pattern derived directly from nature.

What have we got to work with here? Waves as a linear counterweight to reeds. Reeds and waves as disparate elements. Clear design principles in the details, as well as in the whole. Total balance between all parts of the image.

And what about colour? Rhythmic, strong colour values. Unreal effects from the clear green of the

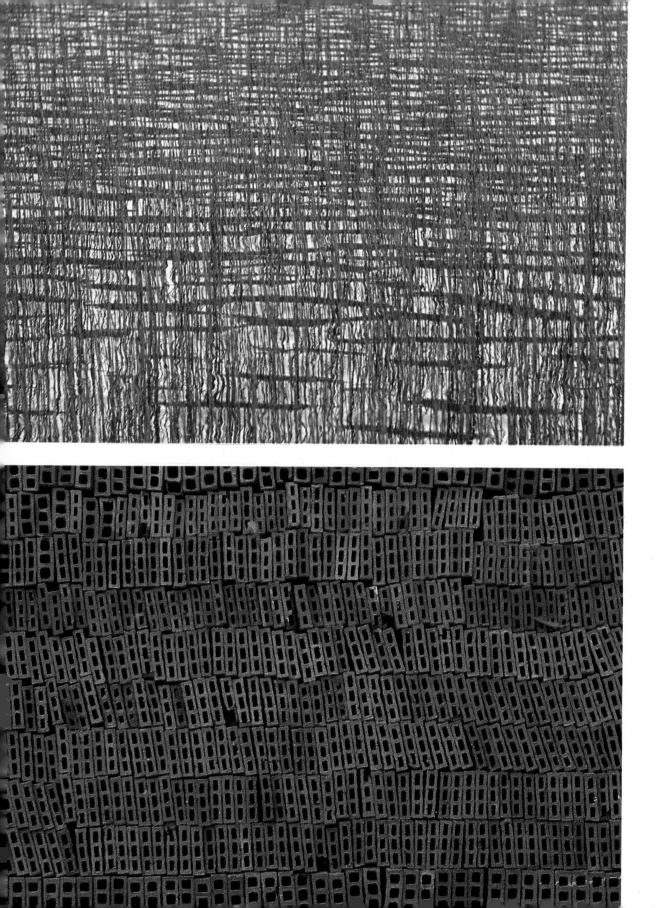

vertical elements. Colour *not* used as an aid to the photographic illusion of three-dimensions.

In the second photo, 'Bricks', the colour contrast is more stabilising and restful. But note again what Mondriaan had to say in the manifesto of 'de Stijl' on the subject of the 'new design': 'clarity, geometry simplicity, the regular, the constructive and the functional.' The horizontals and verticals in this simple pile of bricks have a structure that compels you to look at it, and the irregularities only emphasise the strength of the line and rhythm.

VALUE-FREE–OR VALUELESS?

The type of photograph we have been looking at, using as a motive a fragment from reality the interest of which lies in its form and rhythm, can give rise to considerable discussion on the nature of value-free art. Are these works too formalised, with too little content and giving too little information?

It could be argued that, far from a value-free expression, what we have here is the creation of an abstract through objectivity. Or, to put it even more strongly, reaching the abstract by the complete devaluation of the world of the senses. Perhaps this sounds suspiciously like art for art's sake, like the saying that a well-painted onion is better than a badly-painted madonna.

But are these pictures–these sections of reeds on water, or these stacks of bricks–just value-free or technically fragmentary compositions? Are they no more than the product of calculation and construction? Merely interesting experiments in form? Or are they, in the elitist jargon of the superior art-critic, the *concertised image of the sceptical dementia of transcendent realism?*

To all these questions there is one answer; this is the way in which the photographer uses the material world for the free play of form and colour, working in the abstract and not in any way trying to reproduce a pictorial image. Don't let's get confused with the trickword 'value-free' and the connotation of *valueless*, concluding that such works contain nothing of value, no content and no significance.

What is important about them is not the objective appearance, but the subjective reaction to them. To borrow the words of George Braque, it has to do with 'capitulation before the common appearance of things'. And let Matisse have the last word in this section: 'Nothing should appear in a picture that can be described in words or which already exists in our mind. A picture is a unique organism or it is nothing. When I see a picture, I forget what it is supposed to represent; all that matters is line, form and colour.

REPRODUCTION OR RE-CREATION

Let us get this straight first of all—if there is any such thing as re-creation in photography, it is thanks to reproduction! But, one has to admit that there is and has always been controversy about the nature of photography as an art-form. Take for example this quotation from Hans Heinz Holz, made in the catalogue for Documenta-5 at Kassel in 1972, in the section entitled 'The World of Graphics':–

'The extreme opposite pole at which the graphic (as opposed to the pictorial) becomes mere reproduction is photography, which depicts chance pieces of reality by sheer technical means, without any sort of translation through conscious perception. Although the image produced can be said to be a 'sign' in that it is a representation of a three-dimensional reality, it differs from all other signs in not making an abstraction (!), and in only being subject to technical indistinctness. Indeed, even the explanation of an image *within* the image which can be achieved by the accentuated ability of deliberate reproduction is not possible by technical means. It makes no interpretation, as perception can; it merely records. Despite the widespread use of photography in the modern world, it lacks the capability to reproduce meaning clearly. It is not experienced symbolically . . .

Photography is, as it were, the opposite pole to the sign, in that it merely represents fortuitous or trite segments of reality rather than using abbreviated or distilled forms. Even as art photography, it has to rely on what is depicted and not on the depiction itself.'

Despite all that, this publication of H. H. Holz deserves our attention, and is certainly worth the reading time of any photographer. The only thing wrong with it is the way in which he trots out the same old arguments about photography as a qualitative concept, with all it's misconceptions. Unfortunately, the learned Professor Holz's opinion of photography as mere reproduction without meaning or interpretation only goes to show how little notice he has taken of what the photographic medium has to offer.

If we take a critical look at the illustration on this page, taken from a child's gravestone in Italy, we could say it was merely a photo of a photo, a pure reproduction of something that had been created

previously. On the other hand, it cannot be denied that the recognition and abstraction of this factual situation, the thought processes that went with it, and finally the representation of a pictorial message divorced from the reality, are entirely products of the intellect and creativity of the photographer, and not of some soulless machine.

This weatherbeaten sign from a tradition of naive Christian image and practice has not been put on film as just some technical record of religious articles. It can open up for the beholder a new way of seeing and experiencing things, a way into the territory of dreams, the subconscious. And this has been done, quite seriously, using the style and technique of objective surrealism: a clinically accurate photographic juxtaposition of the portrait of the dead child and the symbols of Christian mythology—the guardian angel and the cross—on this stylised grave.

According to Salvador Dali, a surrealist object (l'objet rouvé) is any 'objet dépaysé'. That is, any object which 'is detached from its usual frame of reference and used for a purpose other than that for which it was originally intended, or for a purpose the outcome of which is unknown.' (Leopold Zahn: Brief History of Modern Art, Ullstein, 1956).

In our example, it is the clear lack of logic in this configuration of impossibilities that produces its inner unity. There is an absurd, alien marriage of opposites made even more unreal by the flecks of weathering and the encrustations of moss on the stone, and the whole is encased in a background, reminiscent of interstellar space. There is a feeling of time, of the fourth dimension or of the 'spritual space' of Henri Matisse.

Anyway, putting all discussion aside, we can surely have no doubt that it is possible that even a photograph which seems at first glance to be mere reproduction can be legitimate in terms of its interpretation of a discovered object, and not simply upon the depiction of it.

CONTENT AND THEME

Today, there is a lot of learned discussion about 'theme' and 'content' without a great deal of understanding of what these terms actually mean. Let us therefore call in the help of the distinguished Czech Professor Antonin Hinst, who has defined these terms as follows:—

Content is the total effect created by the author on the basis of his thoughts, experiences and reflections. The content of a photograph, therefore, is its rational and emotional foundation. Of course, the same picture can have a different content for the author and the viewer since there will always be a difference between what the author intends to express through his subject and how the viewer interprets it.

Theme, on the other hand, is the reality chosen by the author, in the sense of a created reality, and is therefore a real or optically realised image. The concept of theme can thus apply to abstract ideas; you could, for example, combine the representation of a car crash with a view of the soulless monochrome flats that are a feature of the new architecture to express the idea of 'our technical world'. How effective the chosen theme will be depends on the author's talent, his objectives, his experience and, not least, on the technical facilities available to him.

The inspiration that leads to the realisation of a theme need not be identical with the theme itself. The author can be inspired by anything that stimulated him. Even just the creative search approach, without preconceptions, can be a starting point. On the other hand, the author often chooses a theme only after considerable introspection, during the course of which the content of the as-yet-unformed photograph will become apparent to him.

Much less frequently, it arises from an encounter with the unknown, where spontaneously-experienced reality leads directly to a theme and the inspiration for the content becomes available in a fraction of a second.

In conclusion, therefore, we can say that inspiration is the initiation of a chain reaction leading to the general idea of the content and finally to the determination of the theme.

TATTERED ROOFING FELT

With the foregoing conclusions in mind, we will keep the title of the photo on the left as literal as possible. In fact, were we to give it a better, or more artistic title, we might well be treading on dangerous ground. Here, content and the theme of 'erosion' are very close together. The one is indivisibly bonded to the other. The naive viewer might fantasise about this photograph, giving it titles such as 'The Other Side of the Tracks' or 'How the Other Half Lives'. This is fine; everyone has the right to put his own interpretation on things and to see in them what he will. The true meaning of the image does not necessarily have anything to do with the meaning of what it represents.

We can also see the representation as a thing in its own right and value-free, for what meaning can there possibly be in an old bit of tattered roofing felt hanging from some worn-looking planks? Or is there something there? That mysterious fourth dimension of time, perhaps? The viewer always has the last word so you must make up your own minds about it.

For the technically-minded viewer, it was taken with a Leica M3, using Agfachrome 50S Professional, a Hektor 135mm telephoto lens, and an exposure of 1/125 sec at f/5.6.

From a composition point of view, there are two basic forms involved; the plastic form of the felt, and the linear form of the planking. There is a very noticeable contrast between the formlessness of the cladding and the strongly ordered parallelism of the timbering, only visible in the lower half of the picture. Light and dark areas are in balance, especially in the imaginary diagonal formed by the mould patches on the felt at the top right and on the wood at lower left. The line of dark-coloured nail heads at the bottom right form a sort of vertical fence to enclose the image, and the overall monochrome strengthens the impact of this photograph.

INSPIRATION AND REALISATION

Let's look at the photograph first, before discussing the terms. They say a good photo is a gift and we can certainly be thankful when we discover a motive and when everything – form, lighting and colour – comes together to reveal it in all its glory. The picture overleaf is indeed a fortunate photograph of a fascinating landscape with a superb chiaroscuro effect, as well as parallelism, form, contrast and some striking colour contrasts. So inspiration and realisation come together; an attractive subject, ideal lighting conditions, the chance to select a position from which the best view could be obtained and everything needed to bring the composition to successful fruition.

The content of the picture is the overwhelming vastness of nature. The composition starts from the eye-catching peak at the lower left centre sticking up like a hand, but it soon moves on to the pathways of blue and green that wind upwards through the picture, binding it firmly together. The flecks of yellow sunlight which appear in the centre of the picture and again in the background are just sufficient to lift the colouring out of the realism of the sombre, creating a most pleasing effect.

INSPIRATION . . . .

The term 'inspiration' may, for some readers, have unfortunate romantic or sentimental connotations. I would use a word like 'suggestion' if I could, but many of these words are themselves beset with incorrect connotations or are already in use in other disciplines. So let us then simply define 'inspiration' as the instant in which we suddenly feel 'This is it!'

But what is it? What have we got hold of? Content? Theme? Form? Colour? In the photo below, it was form and colour. The questions of theme and content are not so simple. Is the content 'nature's random victims'? Or might the viewer merely see 'danger on the beach'? Is the theme 'beachcombings'? Or shall we move to the world of value-free art, and simply choose to see it as an exercise in colour and form? You can't label everything?

. . . AND REALISATION

This is the 'how' in our study of composition and it tends towards the technical. In other words, which film did we use, what sort of camera and accessories, more especially how did we go about using them and what is our approach to the photo-technical situation? As far as realisation of composition is concerned, of course, we are simply dealing with the factors we have already dealt with before – lines and surfaces, relationships between geometrical points, diagonals as well as lighting and viewpoint including the degree to which detail is included.

149

The Right Time

THE RIGHT PERIOD

To speak of the 'right time' might imply that there is some precise moment in time when a photo is snapped, a once-and-for-all occasion after which the opportunity never comes again. Yet in many cases it is more often a question of the right period – a relatively long span of time over which you take as many photographs as you can possibly manage and later select the best one, or ones.

This was certainly the case in my pigeon photo below. The inspiration came from the dovecote – the attractive colouration and the interesting relationship between horizontal and vertical lines. There were other items of interest as well; the irregularities of the frames and the difference in height between the right and left blinds. Very good, but the problem was the pigeons themselves!

You can't direct pigeons. They went where they wanted to go and not where I wanted them. So I had to wait, and wait and wait for a total of six hours! But, at last, they sat where I wanted them to and I shot off as much film as I could before they moved again. After that, I just had to hope against hope that one of the photographs would be right.

As it turned out, I need not have worried; the two sets of birds were sitting just as if I'd placed them there, and even their 'costumes' had worked out right. However, most important of all, the outermost birds are not looking 'out' of the picture and therefore the composition is held together laterally.

The main feature of this picture is of course its symmetry, with the heavy central axis providing a fulcrum. But it is in the small deviations that much of the interest lies; the drinking bowl in the right-hand house, the different positions of the frames, the strongly rhythmic patterns of the perches at the back, the subtle variations in the colour of the wood, and, not least, the 'actors' themselves, including the 'supervisor' above the head of the centre-left bird.

Patience has its rewards after all!

HOPING FOR THE BEST

As we noted at the very beginning of this book, colour photography is, in effect, writing with reflected, coloured light. And nowhere is there more colour to be reflected at the camera than in the big top. The fascinating events that take place in the circus ring are made even more photogenic by the myriad coloured reflections to be found there. But, at the same time, these very lighting conditions provide a major problem for the photographer who wants to record this strange world of film.

You will have to use the approach described in the previous section. You may also try a fast reflex approach, using a little bit of anticipation, if you dare! But whatever you do, the main problem will always be the exposure. It is of course possible to use flash (if it is allowed) but you will then get a 'realistic' effect and the other-worldliness will be lost. So on these occasions it is very often a matter of leaving your flash behind and hoping for the best.

One way around this is to wait for a suitable sort of lighting (in my case a blue-violet glow) and, setting the shutter to a certain speed, try a number of hand-held shots at different exposures when the lighting looks right. Sharpness no longer matters if you do this, the movement of the horses here is a far greater cause of unsharpness than focusing! You will never be able to know precisely whether you have got a good shot or not but it is a fascinating exercise to try.

If you are successful, as I was here, you will have a fascinating photo indeed, one in which the unreal world of the circus is captured and perhaps even made into something abstract in its own right. The reality gives way before the overwhelming wave of fantasy this photograph evokes; against the concrete colours and shapes of the background we have this mysterious circus ring with its ghostly horses. It is surrounded by a dark ring of spectators, yet they cannot see what the camera saw, a phantom herd from somewhere in the world of dreams.

It was a pity, though, about those kettledrums . . .

EFFECT OF FORMAT

At first sight, this harbour scene looked as though it should be shot in vertical format, with the boats extending away into the background. However, the harbour walls are very important in that they enclose the subject on two sides, so a horizontal format was chosen. Also a wide-angle lens.

There is no need for speed here as in the two previous examples. The fact that the man is standing just where he is most effective as a factor in the total composition is a matter of direction, not fast shooting.

His position is rather critical, nevertheless, since without him the blue boat, because of the property of its blue colouration, would tend to look further away, and the centre of interest of the picture (not the actual centre of course) would tend to shift to the left. The yellow reflection in the water (more a time-dependent factor than any other in this composition) contrasts sharply with the blue of the foreground which itself provides a quality contrast in its various shimmering shades.

The most critical compositional factor of all, though, is the fan-shaped array of the boats themselves, leading to a focal point outside the picture. Here the enclosing harbour walls have a secondary function – they emphasise the slender forms of the boats, as well as the swirling motion that the boats imply. This is also emphasised by the stiff, forward-leaning posture of the man.

The wide-angle lens was an essential element in obtaining the right balance of compositional factors. There is a certain amount of distortion in the shapes of the boats nearest the front of the picture, and this also helped the overall effect.

ETERNAL TRIANGLES

An old married couple and an interloper – a bottle of beer! No words are really needed for this subject – the picture speaks for itself!

There are, however, a couple of compositional points that are worth making. For a start, we have the diagonally reducing size of the three

'models', with the line running almost exactly to the end of the bench. Then there is the eye-catching white plastic bag drawing attention to the huge hands and the pillar-like legs of the wife and contrasting them strongly with the skinny legs and shabby trousers of the miserable little husband. The patch of new brickwork behind his head, the stiff vertical lines of the pipes behind hers . . .

There is a steady growth of shapes as you move from left to right; from nothing to massive in a triangular configuration that gradually fills the frame. A joke? A caricature? Perhaps. More like a little harmless fun or a photographic pun. But most of all, it is an eye-catching picture, something that makes you think and a little slice from life.

There was no question of direction in this photograph. It was essential to avoid giving the couple any feeling of being trapped in any way. It was much more a matter of waiting for just the right moment to take the photo. The moment at which the husband gave a funny little smile, as if at some secret joke of his own. And, with the bottle within reach of his hand, perhaps he had something to smile about!

Finally, just in case any readers are having qualms about the ethics of this photograph, I should say that there was no question of the old couple being exploited in any way. I had asked and received their permission to make this particular triangle immortal, if not eternal.

A ROOF OVER YOUR HEAD

. . . and this house (overleaf), somewhere on the central plateau of Spain, is hardly more than that. A couple of walls, a little window and a thatched roof; yet in its simplicity somehow more of a *house* than many a luxury flat or fashionable pad. This is what attracted me to it.

It was certainly interesting enough at first sight, but there were problems. It was the usual sort of hot, clear day that you get in Spain with not a cloud in the sky to moderate the harsh light of the sun. There were blue shadows under the edge of the roof and everything was far too bright. Initial interest turned to something like despair at an almost impossible situation for a photograph. There was also a sense of challenge; this lighting was *not* going to beat me. And necessity, so they say, is the mother of invention . . .

It then occurred to me that a good way around the problem was to get down to work—literally! With this dramatic lighting, a very low-level shot would make the house stand out like a theatre stage photographed from the stalls. So I lay down on the ground with the camera in front of me and was ready to take the photograph, when suddenly the situation resolved itself. Around the corner came two curious little children, fascinated by the strange and funny man lying on the ground. They stood and stared at me, dumbfounded. Do you speak any Dutch? They didn't even seem to speak Spanish, so flabbergasted were they by the foreigner with all the peculiar apparatus gabbling at them, for I certainly didn't speak Spanish. Impasse. But smiles and gestures are international and soon I had their interest and their trust. And so, showing them that I wanted her hand holding the bowl *there* and his arm around her shoulders *so*, and that he should hold his shirt front like *this* . . . finally, the photograph was taken, to the great relief of all concerned!

They had stood exactly where I wanted them. I didn't want an image of picturesque poverty, but the idea of a house as a roof over the head, as a refuge, is well represented by the children positioned where they are under a merciless sky, with the roof between them, protecting them. On that savage plateau of central Spain, even such a flimsy protection is worth having. The emptiness of the place and the power of the sky are well depicted in the 'empty' right-hand side of the photograph, and now the blue shadows there have a function.

This is no abstract photograph in the style of some of those we have examined in recent pages. It is traditional, perhaps even conventional. In some ways a very simple and straightforward photograph, but at the same time no pretty picture postcard. This is not the sort of place that tourists visit, nor is it the sort of image they look for.

It has a value of its own, nevertheless. We must not fall into the trap of assuming that a thing has to be 'new' to be original. If it is attractive, it is *attractive* whether it is modern or ancient, trailblazing or sedentary and well-known or totally unfamiliar. The newness of things comes in seeing them in a new way with new eyes, for even the most original composition cannot but contain something familiar.

Any photographer who goes out looking for the out-of-the-ordinary, something strange that has never been photographed before, is very likely to miss the real opportunities that lie all around him in the real world. Of course your work must be original, but you must realise that originality lies in seeing the newness in the commonplace and seeing ordinary things in an out-of-the-ordinary way. Photographic originality lies not in what you photograph, but in the way you photograph it. In looking, seeing and handling the subject creatively.

PREPARATION

A prepared snapshot sounds like a contradiction in terms and in many cases it would be. However, you can sometimes create a situation in which a snapshot will be possible; it is therefore the situation that you prepare, and only a fraction of a second of it that you capture.

In this case, there was certainly time to prepare. I had been sighting through my viewfinder for quite a while but it wasn't quite right. There was certainly plenty of action so I had been able to select a position that gave maximum expression to the group and the intensity with which its members were working. But the hard quality of the backlighting, together with the dark background, seemed to compress the people and the earth they were working into one solid clod, and that I didn't want.

Then came the right moment we have been talking about – in the form of the tractor and the cloud of dust that accompanied it. Suddenly the harsh lighting was diffused by the dust cloud which also obscured much of the background, giving life and three-dimensionality to the group and the scene. Then, just as I was ready, the boy at the right raised his arm and suddenly all the figures in shot were interconnected.

There is a considerable element of light-dark contrast in this picture, and this was one of the many things that became apparent later to reinforce the conclusion that it had indeed been taken at exactly the right moment. For the dust cloud had diffused the light enough to produce a silhouette effect all over the picture, while at the same time softening details and lightening shadows.

If we just look at this picture, ignoring the atmospheric effects, we can see it as just a direct and unpretentious record of a place, a time and a process. It is not some objective and timelessly realistic social document; and still less is it an illusion of idyllic rural life. It manages to avoid the 'blood and soil' image, too. It is simply an unromantic look at working people, and a title like 'The Potato Harvest' would be entirely suitable for it.

In this respect, it has something in common with the paintings of the French realists Courbet and Millet who managed so well to depict the theme of people at work without sentimentality. And it is from these painters that we might re-emphasise one of the constantly recurring points of this book; that of seeing photographically. Courbet himself once said 'Paint only what you see!' For 'paint' read 'photograph'.

LIFE IS A CAROUSEL

What to one person is just a fairground roundabout or something from which to make a pretty picture, to another might be the subject of something deeper.

So the creative photographer looking for a means of expression for his theme, might seek an unusual viewpoint or a very high aspect from which the carousel forms an interesting double circle in the centre of the image-field. There, he might wait until a group of people are kind enough to arrange themselves in a suitable configuration at the right, conveniently balancing out the composition for him. And if he thinks the lower circle too empty and too cold-looking, he might just wait until the showman himself steps on to it. Deliberate composition or just good luck?

Or, even better – what are you really trying to do? The circle is the dominant shape but it is less interesting than the contrast with the sober white wagon which accompanies it. The 'spiral arm' of spectators bracketing the roundabout gives em-

phasis to the basic form; it is hardly recognisable as a group of people because of the distance. So one answer is to be found in the earlier discussion we had about theme and content; what the author sees in his work may not be what the viewer sees. That more or less answers the second question.

What about the other? There's a lot said about the aims of photography today. The 'negation of aesthetics' and 'superbanality' have become accepted as basics of modern artistic expression. But that sort of verbal chatter cannot cover up faulty workmanship.

To be up-to-date or progressive, does not mean that you have to produce meaningless documentation. To be modern and austere and to clear out the clutter of unwanted prejudices from the past does not mean that you have to throw out the baby with the bathwater. For the serious photographer, it must always be important for his work to be aesthetically and compositionally in balance.

So, to return to our example for a final comment, the point of this picture is not really to explain that the photographer thinks that life is just a carousel; but it has a lot more to do with his way of seeing forms, which is what the next and final chapter of this book is all about.

PLANNING AND LUCK

For natural drama, there are few places on the surface of the planet to beat Iceland. Here we have a photo of that most breathtaking spectacle, a geyser blowing its jet of water and steam high up against a stormy northern sky.

The photographic representation of this mysterious force presents interesting problems. For a start, the geyser is irregular; it spouts when it feels like it! Then there is the force of the stormy wind to reckon with, as well as the fact that, at this time of year, even the midnight sky in Iceland is light and bluish in colour.

Hardest of all, however, is timing. There is an instant when the whole mass of water hangs motionless in the air before falling back to earth. It is therefore a matter of pure calculation to discover the exposure which will allow the shutter to open just before the highest point is reached and to close before the jet begins to fall back again. Too short an exposure will freeze the jet, destroying the impression of motion which is essential to the nature of the subject.

And this is where luck comes in. Out of a dozen or more shots, this last one produced the picture I wanted. It is the optimum, the universal picture of a geyser. For, just at the moment when the shutter was open, the full force of the storm wind caught the hovering water-mass, slamming it away to the left against a clearing that only a second before had begun to appear in the angry sky.

The force of the wind is almost tangible in the tatters to the right of the enormous mass of water and steam; they act like the streamlines used for indicating motion in drawings. The heavy upward diagonal of the skyline is crossed by the slanting line of the geyser jet, and the dominant colours of purple, green and blue add a final touch of drama to this already dramatic subject.

FORM AND DESIGN

It is not by chance that the subject of form has been left to the end of this book. Of all the terms we have come across, it is by far the hardest to define. Indeed, it was many years before I had any real notion of what this concept meant.

Of course we know what form means you reply. Just look in the dictionary! So let's look. 'Form', says the dictionary, is 'the shape or configuration of something . . . . the particular mode, appearance etc. in which a thing manifests itself'. But this doesn't really help. These definitions are not concrete. There's not a lot you can do with them, especially in the field of creative colour photography.

What about 'design'? From the same source, we have 'the arrangement or pattern of elements or features in an artistic or decorative work'. But this hasn't got a lot to do with form. The elements of a photo could be lines or surfaces, or even spots of colour. So design is an active concept, whereas form is passive.

For the purposes of this book, about the best definition we can achieve is: 'Form is the way something looks to us, or the way in which we make it appear'. Or we can say: 'Form is what a subject communicates to us because of its linear or spatial effect'. Or perhaps even, 'Form is that which enables a thing to be recognisable and to have its own significance among other things'. And that's about as far as we dare go in trying to tie down such an elusive concept as form, especially of form as a motive in the processes of creative design.

Form As Motive

FORM AS MOTIVE

Form need not be three-dimensional. It can appear as simple beauty, as value-free aesthetics or as something dredged up from the strange world of the subconscious. Form must be uncovered; you must be drawn to it and go along with it.

For that, I have to thank my late and much-lamented friend, the great photographer Meinard Woldringh, who died before his time and had an important posthumous exhibition in 1969 at the Leiden Lakenhal. As well as being my friend, he was also my teacher and his work has always been a great stimulus for me, especially in the difficult area of form as motive.

CIRCLES AND LINES

This is a very simple yet striking example of form in two dimensions. The essential contrast is between the two most fundamental aspects of form—the circle and the line. Rhythm and parallelism play a part in this composition, as does the complementary contrast between the colours green and blue. Here, form and design (strongly geometric design at that) go hand in hand.

FORM AND FORMAT

This vertical window flanked by two vertical pillars is, you might think at first, a subject for vertical format. Yet it is not, compositionally. We have therefore gone for 6 × 6cm. But it is not just a spirit of compromise that leads to this choice. It is chiefly because it is only this way that we can arrive at a satisfactory division of surfaces. If you look more closely, you will see that it is not only the vertical that makes this subject what it is. There are also strong horizontal elements, especially the broad band that acts as a foundation for the whole picture. Also, the choice of format allows us to achieve a satisfactory colour balance; vertical format would allow the blue of the blind to catch the eye too much, taking it away from the beautiful green designs on the tiled walls. Even the apparent distraction of the grey patch at the left is important, as is also the asymmetry of the verticals.

BOATS IN THE ICE

Form, colour and composition are the hallmarks of this photograph. The lines shooting from left to right, enclosed by the gunwales of the sunken boats, are the main design elements. There is also of course, the complementary colour contrast between the hulls and the ice; also within the same elements, a simultaneous cold-warm contrast. The forms are bright and clear and they indicate more than is actually visible, reaching beyond the reality of the scene to imply something else.

JELLYFISH

Another circular theme, but this time with a
certain amount of depth. Form and colour were
the inspiration for this photograph; the way in
which the trailing tentacles break into the
rounded form of this dead creature is of great
importance to the composition. In this example,
form is identical with content.

COASTAL SNOWSCAPE–1

Although the subject is an obvious one for the telephoto lens, I used a wide-angle here. The dynamic nature of the scene is reduced and the waves of the snowfield are compacted into solid forms. Repetition is not the starting point here, as might otherwise be the case; the basis of the photograph is sheer form.

COASTAL SNOWSCAPE–2

A pile of plastic shapes, made up of a mixture of drifting snow and sand. The snowstorm has driven across the scene from right to left, leaving snow lying on the lee slopes. This gives a wave-motion effect, apparently moving in the opposite direction, delineated by dynamic streamlines. The compositional approach is meant to emphasise the abstract forms, but at the same time the landscape impression is retained.

COASTAL SNOWSCAPE–3

Once again, the wide-angle lens has been used, and it shows how the judicious choice of camera position can be a critical factor in photographic composition. The lens pulls the foreground towards the camera, pushing the background further away, and a world reminiscent of the work of Tanguy is created; a study in form *per se*.

IN CONCLUSION

Perhaps it might be a good thing if, at the end of this final chapter, the interested reader were to go back and re-read the section entitled 'An Introduction to Design'. It is probable that, after following through all the text and examples, the design exercises given there will be a lot more meaningful and useful. They should widen and deepen the concept of form which I hope this book has managed to instil. There is no substitute for doing things yourself; as a method of learning it is infinitely better than any amount of reading or listening.

The aim of the book is to give a better insight into the techniques of colour photography and, in particular, to introduce the reader to the grammar of the language of photographic composition.

If this enables any reader to give greater rein to his own creativity through the medium of photography, it will be a matter of great satisfaction for me, as well as a stimulus to go ahead on my own chosen path.